checkp■int

Endorsed by
University of Cambridge
International Examinations

biology

Peter D Riley

Hodder Murray

A MEMBER OF THE HODDER HEADLINE GROUP

Titles in this series

Checkpoint Biology Pupil's Book	ISBN 978 0 7195 8067 3
Checkpoint Biology Teacher's Resource Book	ISBN 978 0 7195 8068 0
Checkpoint Chemistry Pupil's Book	ISBN 978 0 7195 8065 9
Checkpoint Chemistry Teacher's Resource Book	ISBN 978 0 7195 8066 6
Checkpoint Physics Pupil's Book	ISBN 978 0 7195 8069 7
Checkpoint Physics Teacher's Resource Book	ISBN 978 0 7195 8070 3

To Tabitha Grace

Orders: please contact Bookpoint Ltd, 130 Milton Park, Abingdon, Oxon OX14 4SB. Tel: (44) 01235 827720. Fax: (44) 01235 400454. Lines are open from 9.00–5.00, Monday to Saturday, with a 24-hour message answering service. Visit our websites www.hoddereducation.co.uk and www.hoddersamplepages.co.uk

© Peter Riley 2005
First published in 2005
by Hodder Murray, an imprint of Hodder Education,
a member of the Hodder Headline Group, an Hachette Livre UK Company
338 Euston Road
London NW1 3BH

Impression number   10 9 8 7 6 5 4
Year   2010 2009 2008 2007

Cover design John Townson/Creation
Typeset in 12/14pt Garamond Light by Pantek Arts Ltd, Maidstone, Kent
Printed in Italy

A CIP catalogue record for this title is available from the British Library

ISBN-13 978 0 719 58067 3

Contents

Preface

To the pupil

Biology is the scientific study of living things. It includes investigations on tiny structures, such as cells, and on huge structures, such as a rainforest, an ocean or even the whole Earth! Some biologists are even looking for signs of life in other parts of the Solar System or on planets around other stars.

Our knowledge of biology has developed from the observations, investigations and ideas of many people over a long period of time. Today this knowledge is increasing more rapidly as there are more biologists – people who study living things – than ever before.

In the past, few people other than scientists were informed about the latest discoveries. Today, through newspapers, television and the Internet, everyone can learn about the latest discoveries on a wide range of biological topics, from curing illnesses and developing new food to ways of reducing environmental damage and conserving rare species.

Checkpoint Biology covers the requirements of your examinations in a way that I hope will help you understand how observations, investigations and ideas have led to the scientific facts we use today. The questions are set to help you extract information from what you read and see, and to help you think more deeply about each chapter in this book. Some questions are set so you can discuss your ideas with others and develop a point of view on different scientific issues. This should help you in the future when new scientific issues, which are as yet unknown, affect your life.

The scientific activities of thinking up ideas to test and carrying out investigations are enjoyed so much by many people that they take up a career in science. Perhaps *Checkpoint Biology* may help you to take up a career in science too.

To the teacher

Checkpoint Biology has been developed from *Biology Now! 11–14* second edition to specially cover the requirements of the University of Cambridge International Examinations Checkpoint tests and other equivalent junior secondary science courses.

It also has the following aims:

- to help pupils become more scientifically literate by encouraging them to examine the information in the text and illustrations in order to answer questions about it in a variety of ways. For example, *For discussion* questions may be used in work on science and citizenship
- to present science as a human activity by considering the development of scientific ideas from the earliest times to the present day
- to examine applications of scientific knowledge, and the issues that arise from them.

This *Pupil's Book* begins with an introduction which briefly reviews the development of science, and in particular biology, throughout the world, and then moves on to consider the scientific method and its applications. As many consequences of scientific work raise issues, the introduction concludes by addressing an issue with a biological base, and it shows strategies that pupils can use to consider the problems and to try and resolve them. These strategies can be used in the rest of the book in discussion activities where issues with a biological base arise.

The chapters are arranged in the order of the topics in the Cambridge Checkpoint Biology Scheme of Work. Chapters 1–5 address topics for Year 1, Chapters 6–10 address topics for Year 2 and Chapters 11–15 address topics for Year 3.

There is an extensive glossary at the back of the book which includes all the words designated in each topic as essential to the pupil's scientific vocabulary.

This *Pupil's Book* is supported by a *Teacher's Resource Book* that provides answers to all the questions in the pupil's book – those that occur in the body of the chapter and those that occur as end-of-chapter questions. It also provides end-of-chapter tests, which can be used for extra assessment, and actual questions from past Checkpoint tests. There is a range of practical activities for integration with the work in each chapter to provide opportunities for students to develop their skills in scientific investigation.

Acknowledgements

Cover and **p.i** John Townson/Creation; **p.1** NASA/Science Photo Library; **p.2** © Robert Campbell/Corbis Sygma; **p.3** © Wolfgang Kaehler/Corbis; **p.4** Mark de Fraeye/Science Photo Library; **p.5** Philippe Psaila/ Science Photo Library; **p.8** *t* Dr Morley Read/Science Photo Library, *b* Renee Lynn/Science Photo Library; **p.10** Peter Chadwick/Science Photo Library; **p.11** Claude Nuridsany & Marie Perennou/Science Photo Library; **p.12** *t* Claude Nuridsany & Marie Perennou/Science Photo Library, *b* © Breck P. Kent/Earth Scenes/Oxford Scientific Films; **p.14** Martin Dohrn/Science Photo Library; **p.15** Claude Nuridsany & Marie Perennou/Science Photo Library; **p.16** *t* Dr Jeremy Burgess/Science Photo Library, *b* Peter Chadwick/Science Photo Library; **p.26** Fred McConnaughey/Science Photo Library, **p.27** Lee White/Corbis; **p.29** © Tom & Dee Ann McCarthy/Corbis; **p.32** G.I. Bernard/NHPA; **p.36** J.C. Revy/Science Photo Library; **p.46** *t* Robert Pickett/Corbis, *b* Microfield Scientific Ltd/Science Photo Library; **p.48** *tl* © Michael & Patricia Fogden/Corbis, *tr* Andrew J. Martinez/Science Photo Library, *bl* Bettmann/Corbis, *br* Richard Cummins/Corbis; **p.49** *t* Georgette Douwma/Science Photo Library *bl* Peter Scoones/Science Photo Library, *br* Tom McHugh/Science Photo Library; **p.50** Andrew Brown/Science Photo Library; **p.51** Heather Angel; **p.52** Dan Guravich/Science Photo Library; **p.58** *t* Heather Angel, *l* Andrew Henley/Natural Visions, *r* Jany Sauvanet/NHPA; **p.60** Tom & Dee Ann McCarthy/Corbis; **p.61** © Kelly-Mooney Photography/Corbis; **p.62** *l* Ron Giling/Lineair/Still Pictures, *r* A. Crump, TDR, WHO/Science Photo Library; **p.64** © Wolfgang Kaehler/Corbis; **p.66** John Hawkins/Frank Lane Picture Agency; **p.68** *t* George Ranalli/Science Photo Library, *b* Martin Bond/Science Photo Library; **p.69** *l* Neil McIntyre, *r* Allan G. Potts/Bruce Coleman Ltd; **p.70** Tom McHugh/Science Photo Library; **p.71** © James L. Amos/Corbis; **p.72** Harwood/Ecoscene; **p.73** *t* Sally Morgan/Ecoscene, *b* © Jacomina Wakeford; **p.78** Art Wolfe/Science Photo Library; **p.79** © Royalty-Free/Corbis; **p.80** *t* G.I. Angel, *b* Natural Visions/Heather Angel; **p.81** *t* Simon Fraser/Science Photo Library, *b* © Keren Su/Corbis; **p.82** Simon Fraser/Science Photo Library; **p.83** *t* George Post/Science Photo Library, *b* David Woodfall/NHPA; **p.84** Stephen Dalton/NHPA; **p.85** *t* Doug Allan/Science Photo Library, *b* Fred Bavendam/Still Pictures; **p.86** Dr Jeremy Burgess/Science Photo Library; **p.92** Andrew Lambert; **p.95** Biophoto Associates/Science Photo Library; **p.97** Heather Angel; **p.106** *t* Royal College of Physicians Photo Library, *b* Jason Venus/Natural Visions; **p.116** Biophoto Associates/Science Photo Library; **p.118** Wellcome Institute, London; **p.120** Damien Lovegrove/Science Photo Library; **p.126** Deep Light Productions/Science Photo Library; **p.130** © Morton Beebe, S.F./Corbis; **p.135** Holt Studios/Nigel Cattlin; **p.137** © Caroline Penn/Corbis; **p.139** John Durham/Science Photo Library; **p.140** Sinclair Stammers/Science Photo Library; **p.142** *l* Duncan Smith/Science Photo Library, *r* Holt Studios/Nigel Cattlin; **p.143** *l* Adrian T Sumner/Science Photo Library, *r* Paul Harcourt Davies/Science Photo Library; **p.146** Heather Angel; **p.152** Harry Smith Horticultural Photographic Collection; **p.154** Stefan Meyers/Ardea London Ltd; **p.156** © Juliet Hignet/Hutchinson Library; **p.157** All: Holt Studios/Nigel Cattlin; **p.164** Eye of Science/Science Photo Library; **p.165** Kenneth H. Thomas/Science Photo Library; **p.166** Stephen Dalton/NHPA; **p.167** *t* Stephen Dalton/NHPA, *cl* Oxford Scientific Films/Dr J.A.L. Cooke, *cr* Stephen Dalton/NHPA, *b* Stephen Dalton/NHPA; **p.168** *t* © Wildlife Matters, *cl* Paul Simons/Biophotos, *cr* Harry Smith Horticultural Photographic Collection; **p.171** *t* © Garden World Images, *b* © copyright the Board of Trustees of the Royal Botanic Gardens, Kew; **p.173** © Jeff Foot/nature.com; **p.174** *t* Dale Boyer/Science Photo Library, *b* Michel Rauch/Still Pictures; **p.175** *t* Michel Rauch/Still Pictures, *b* © Richard Davies/Oxford Scientific Films; **p.176** © Reuters/Corbis; **p.177** BDI Images; **p.178** Michael P. Gadomski/Science Photo Library; **p.179** Tom McHugh/Science Photo Library; **p.186** © Wildlife Matters; **p.189** Peter Scoones/Science Photo Library; **p.190** Adrian T Sumner/Science Photo Library; **p.191** Art Wolfe/Science Photo Library; **p.192** Dr Morley Read/Science Photo Library; **p.193** © Fritz Polking; Frank Lane Picture Agency/Corbis; **p.195** *t* Gregory Dimijan/Science Photo Library, *b* Claude Muridsany & Marie Peremmou/Science Photo Library; **p.196** Adam Hart-Davis/Science Photo Library; **p.197** Gregory Dimijian/Science Photo Library; **p.198** © Pete Oxford/nature.com; **p.199** Gerard Lacz/Still Pictures; **p.201** *t* Associated Press, *b* Simon Fraser/Science Photo Library; **p.204** Mary Evan Picture Library; **p.205** *l* Giles Angel/Natural Visions, *r* John Townson/Creation; **p.208** Heather Angel; **p.209** Hulton Archive; **p.210** *t* Geoscience Features Picture Library, *b* Ecoscene/Alexandra Jones; **p.211** Ecoscene/Kieran Murray; **p.213** Phillip Wallick/Agstock/Science Photo Library; **p.215** Holt Studios/Nigel Cattlin; **p.219** *l* Holt Studios/Bob Gibbons, *r* Holt Studios/Nigel Cattlin; **p.222** M.I. Walker/Science Photo Library; **p.223** P.H. Plailly/Eurelios/Science Photo Library.

t = top, *b* = bottom, *l* = left, *r* = right, *c* = centre

Every effort has been made to contact copyright holders but if any have been inadvertently overlooked the Publishers will be pleased to make the necessary arrangements at the earliest opportunity.

Introduction

The Earth as seen from Apollo 11 showing clear skies over North Africa on the left.

As far as we know, this planet is not like any other. It is the home of living things. The chances are that there are other planets in the universe with living things on them, we just have not discovered them yet. Perhaps we may even find living things on nearby Mars, during your lifetime.

When scientists look for life on other worlds they look for water. You can see in the photograph above that the Earth has large areas covered with water. It is in the water that about 3.6 billion years ago living things are thought to have formed. From there they spread onto the land and into the air. Today scientists talk about a living layer covering the Earth's surface. They call this layer the biosphere. The biosphere is composed of all the plants and animals and microbes on the Earth, and it reaches from beneath the ocean floor to high in the air. You are sitting in the biosphere right now as you read these words. What other living things are around you?

The first biologists

Our knowledge of living things has built up from the earliest people who lived on the Earth, almost two million years ago. These people survived by hunting animals and gathering fruits, nuts and roots. They used a vital scientific process to do this – they made observations. From their observations they learnt which plant foods were safe to eat and which were poisonous. By observing animals they discovered how animals behaved – where they liked to go to eat or drink water. From these observations the hunters could plan where to go to make their attacks, and not waste time and energy looking for their prey all over the surrounding countryside.

About ten thousand years ago people began growing plants for food instead of just searching for them in the countryside. This required other skills beside observation. Investigations had to be made on the growth of plants, such as how close together plants should be grown and whether the plants should be grown in sunlight or in the shade. Failure to discover these facts would mean a failed crop and hunger.

The first human fossils were found in Africa at a site like this one.

Over the next few thousand years a wide range of plants were grown for food in many different places on the planet. Potatoes were grown in Peru, rice in India and China, wheat in Turkey, sugar cane in New Guinea, bananas, coconuts and yams in Indonesia, maize, beans, peppers and squash in Mexico, and millet in Africa.

A wide variety of food is available because farmers in the past found successful ways to grow crops. These vegetables are for sale at a market in Delhi, India.

Science moves on

Once people started farming they could settle down and live in one place. In time, towns and even cities developed. People collected their knowledge of the world and wrote it down. In Greece about two and a half thousand years ago there were places of learning, rather like universities today, which were run by teachers called philosophers. They tried to explain their observations by reasoning and arguing their ideas with others. Most of the Greek philosophers did not believe in testing their ideas with investigations. Even so, most people believed what they said and wrote it down.

About twelve hundred years ago most of the study of science passed to Muslim countries in Africa and Asia. The Muslim scientists were not content with many of the explanations of the Greek philosophers, and began testing their ideas with scientific investigations. Their work led to the setting up of medicine as a science, and in many Muslim cities there were hospitals to care for the sick.

Greek philosophers arguing instead of investigating.

About four hundred years ago most of the study of science passed to European countries. Scientific investigations were carried out following the ideas of the Muslim scientists such as Mohammad Ibn Zakariya al-Razi (864–930), and developed by Francis Bacon (1561–1626) in England. The way to tackle a scientific investigation became known as the scientific method.

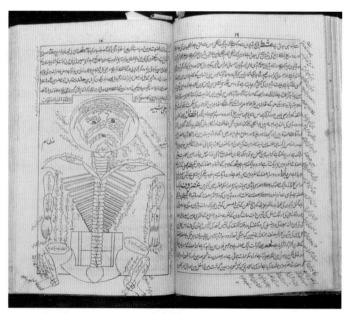

A historical medical textbook from the Indian subcontinent.

The scientific method

In the scientific method an observation is made and then an idea, called a hypothesis, is developed from the observation. An experiment is then made to test the hypothesis. The results of the experiment are collected and studied to see if they agree or disagree with the hypothesis. There is no right or wrong answer, just a result to consider against a hypothesis. From this consideration a conclusion can be drawn and a new piece of knowledge might be discovered.

Try the scientific method with this activity.

Observation

Many plants release seeds into the air. When the seed falls to the ground it can come to rest in any position – on its side, right way up or upside down.

Hypothesis

Does the way a seed rests on the ground stop it from sprouting?

Seeds being released from a spinning top conebush. The seeds can be dispersed many kilometres on the wind.

Experiment

1 Take some soaked broad bean seeds and plant them in different positions as the diagram shows.

2 After a week carefully dig up the seeds and see if they have sprouted.

Results

Make a drawing of each seed after a week and compare the results with the hypothesis. The hypothesis suggests that some of the seeds will not sprout because of the way they are lying. Do your results show this?

Conclusion

From comparing your results with the hypothesis what do you conclude? Does the way a seed rests on the ground affect the way it sprouts, or do seeds sprout in any position?

What has happened here?

The result of an experiment can be used to explain other observations. When you have completed the experiment on sprouting seeds use your results to explain what has happened to this seedling.

By using the scientific method scientists have discovered a huge number of facts. Many biological facts in this book have been discovered this way, and today scientists still use the scientific method in their research work.

For discussion
What kinds of biological research do you think are being carried out today? Check your ideas by finding out what biological research is being done at the university nearest to your school. Log onto their website and look for the biology department web pages.

Issues

Some of the facts that have been discovered through scientific investigation can be used to help us survive – through helping us grow crops more efficiently or making medicines to treat disease. Scientific facts can also help when dealing with many issues in everyday life. When people have different ideas about solving a problem, the problem becomes an issue. A very simple issue could be your homework. You want to do it at a certain time and members of your family want you to do it at another time. How do you resolve this issue?

On page 8 is an imaginary example of an issue in which science facts can be helpful. Read about it then try the exercises in dealing with the issue.

Consequence map

One way of considering an issue is to make a consequence map.

Use _ _ _ _ _ to indicate a positive consequence.
Use ———— to indicate a negative consequence.
Use .... to indicate an opinion.

Some consequences have been done already to help you start making your map (see below). Think up some more consequences and add them to the map.

The rainforest is made into a national park.

_ _ _ _ _ The rare animal is protected.
———— Apa has to change his way of life.
.... The rainforest will look better.

A rare animal is protected.

For discussion
Read the story to your friends and present your consequence map. Ask for their views and discuss them. Is the issue resolved satisfactorily?

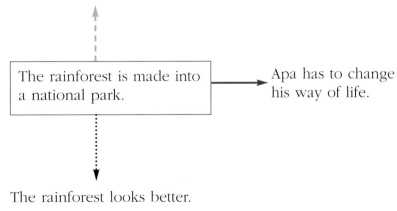

The rainforest is made into a national park.

Apa has to change his way of life.

The rainforest looks better.

Apa lives in a rainforest with his family. They hunt a few animals and collect some fruits, but they also grow crops. They do this by cutting down a few trees and burning away the undergrowth to make space for their plants. After a few years all the nutrients in the soil (called minerals) are used up by the crop plants, and Apa and his family move on and clear a new space. Rainforest plants grow back in the space they leave behind. Apa's family have lived this way for generations. It is their traditional way of life and they are happy to continue living in this way.

This rainforest is being cleared to grow crops. The trees will not be allowed to grow back.

Two people arrive at Apa's home. Obe works for the government of the country. She tells Apa that scientific research has shown that the rainforest is the home of an animal that is in danger of becoming extinct. The government has decided that the rainforest should be made a national park, and that Apa and his family must move to the edge of it and live there.

Camemono is to be the new park ranger. He tells Apa that the only people who will be allowed in the park are tourists. They will only visit with Camemono's men and will pay to make their trip. The money raised by tourists will help to conserve the rare animal, and perhaps increase its numbers.

Apa does not want to give up his way of life. Obe and Camemono want Apa to move out of the forest. Can a solution be found to this issue?

The ocelot is a very rare rainforest mammal.

Goals, rights and responsibilities

The issue can be examined by looking at the goals, rights and responsibilities of the people involved. A goal is what a person wants to achieve. A right is a person's entitlement to being treated in a particular way no matter what the consequence. A responsibility is a person's obligation to act in a particular way.

Here is a suggestion for the goals, rights and responsibilities of Apa. Try and think of more and add them to the lists.

Goal – to help himself and his family survive.
Right – a place to live.
Responsibility – to provide a home for his family.

What are the goals, rights and responsibilities of Obe and Camemono?

You may like to use consequence maps and consider goals, rights and responsibilities when working on other issues in this book.

For discussion

Present your lists of goals, rights and responsibilities to your friends. Ask for their views and discuss them. Is the issue resolved satisfactorily?

♦ SUMMARY ♦

♦ The living layer covering the Earth is called the biosphere (*see page 1*).

♦ Early people used their powers of observation to help them find food (*see page 2*).

♦ Simple investigations on plant growth helped early farmers raise crops (*see page 2*).

♦ The Ancient Greeks tried to explain their observations without making investigations (*see page 3*).

♦ Muslim scientists carried out investigations to help explain their observations (*see page 3*).

♦ The scientific method is used in investigations today (*see page 5*).

♦ Issues involving science can be studied by making consequence maps (*see page 7*).

♦ Issues involving science can be studied by considering goals, rights and responsibilities of people (*see page 9*).

---

1 Characteristics of living things

Figure 1.1 Klipspringers spend the hottest part of the day resting among rocks.

1 How is a living thing different from something that has never lived?

You can make two groups of things – living things and things that have never lived. These klipspringers are living things, but the rock they are standing on has never lived.

> For discussion
>
> If you grouped things into living things and things that have never lived, where would you place a block of wood?

Signs of life

If something is called a living thing it must have seven special features. These are called the characteristics of life. The characteristics are feeding, respiring, moving, growing, excreting (getting rid of waste), reproduction, and irritability (being sensitive to the surroundings).

Animal life

2 Which characteristics of life are shown by the mice in the pictures A–D in Figure 1.2?

3 Does
   a) an aeroplane,
   b) a computer,
   c) a brick have any characteristics of life? Explain your answers.

All animals have the same seven characteristics of life but they may show them in different ways. For example, some animals have a skeleton on the outside of the

A

B

C

D

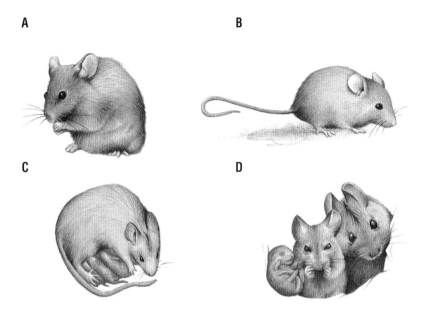

Figure 1.2   Four of the characteristics of life.

body and can grow only when they shed the old skeleton and stretch a new soft skeleton beneath before it sets. Insects and spiders do this by taking in air. Crabs and lobsters stretch their new skeletons by taking in water. Animals with skeletons inside their bodies simply grow larger without having to shed their skeletons.

Figure 1.3   This desert locust is shedding its last skeleton. Here the wings are rolled together, forming an arch on the locust's back.

Living things use oxygen to respire. Many animals living on land have lungs in which they take oxygen from the air. Many aquatic animals have gills which take up oxygen dissolved in the water.

Figure 1.4 The axolotl's gills are on the outside of its body behind its head.

Plant life

Green plants also have the same seven features but they show them in different ways to animals. Plants make food from oxygen in the air and water by using energy from sunlight. Chemicals in the soil are also needed, but in very small amounts. All plant cells respire and gaseous exchange takes place through their leaves.

Figure 1.5 Seedlings growing towards the light.

4 How is a green plant's way of feeding different from an animal's way of feeding?

Plants move as they grow and can spread out over the ground. Wastes may also be stored in the leaves. Green plants are sensitive to light and grow towards it. Plants reproduce by making seeds or spores. Some plants reproduce by making copies of themselves.

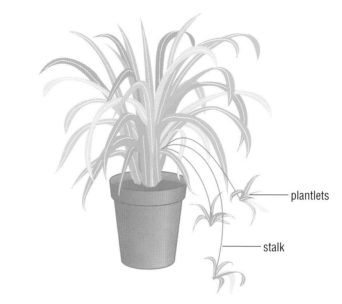

Figure 1.6 A spider plant makes plantlets on stalks.

plantlets

stalk

For discussion

A car can have five characteristics of life. What are they and how does the car show them?

If there are drought conditions, why might a plant produce seeds rather than grow new plantlets?

Life on Mars?

In 1976 two Viking spacecraft reached Mars. When they arrived each spacecraft split in two. One part, called the Orbiter, travelled around the planet taking photographs and measuring temperatures. The second part, called the Lander, touched down on the planet's surface. Although the Lander measured the Martian weather and had equipment on board to detect vibrations like earthquakes, the experiments that everyone wanted to know about were the ones to test the soil for signs of life. There was great excitement when one of the soil samples began to froth. It could have been caused by something respiring – a sign of life. After a few weeks of further investigation it was decided that the froth was most probably made by a chemical reaction not connected to a living organism.

There are signs that water once ran over the planet's surface, so some scientists believe that there could still be life there, but that it is buried deeper in the soil than the Lander could reach.

In 1997 the Pathfinder probe reached Mars and a vehicle called the Sojourner travelled around the landing site to take photographs and perform tests on rocks. It did not have any experiments on board to test for life.

Further observations on the planet have shown that some water is present. As living things need water there is a chance that when the water is examined some life forms may be found.

1 What were the two parts of the Viking spacecraft and what did each part do?
2 Why could the froth be a sign that something was respiring?
3 What are the advantages and disadvantages of bringing back Martian rock to Earth to look for organisms?
4 Can any of the disadvantages be overcome? Explain your answer.

13

Looking at signs of life

Eating and feeding

5 How many different kinds of food do you eat?

All living things need food. Plants make their own food but animals must get it from other living things. Some animals, like ourselves, eat a wide range of foods, while others eat only a small range of foods.

In the rainforest ticks, lice, leeches and mosquitoes feed on one food – blood. They have mouths which can break through skin and suck up their meal.

Figure 1.7 These leeches are being used for medicinal purposes.

6 How is the mouth of a crocodile adapted for feeding?

Every animal has a mouth which is specially developed or adapted for the animal to feed in a particular way.

Respiration

Respiration is the process in which energy is released from food. The released energy is used for life processes such as growth and movement. Respiration takes place in the bodies of both plants and animals. It is a chemical reaction. During respiration, a food called glucose reacts with oxygen to release energy, and carbon dioxide and water are produced. The word equation for this chemical reaction is:

glucose + oxygen → carbon dioxide + water

Respiration should not be confused with breathing, which is the process of moving air in and out of the body (see page 23). Later when you study how plants make food you must remember that while the plants are making food in a process called photosynthesis they are also respiring to stay alive.

Movement

Let your right arm hang down by your chair. Stick the fingers of your left hand into the skin in the upper part of your right arm (above the forearm). Raise your right forearm and you should feel the flesh in the upper arm become harder. It is muscle, and it is working to move your forearm upwards. Muscles provide movement for all animals. Animals move to find food, avoid enemies and find shelter. Even when an animal is sitting or standing still, muscles are at work. On page 23 you can see that the diaphragm muscle helps you to breathe, and there are muscles between your ribs that move them up and down. Inside your body your heart muscle pumps blood around the body, and muscles in the wall of your stomach churn up your food to help it digest.

Irritability

Animals detect or sense changes in their surroundings by their sense organs. These are the skin, eye, ear, tongue and nose. Some animals such as insects and centipedes have long antennae, which they use to touch the ground in front of them. The information their brains receive helps them decide if it is safe to move forwards.

Figure 1.8 The weevil has a long proboscis and antennae to sense changes in the surroundings.

Figure 1.9 This snake is collecting chemicals in the air with its forked tongue.

Like many animals we use our eyes and ears to tell us a great deal about our surroundings. We use our tongue and nose to provide us with information about food. If it smells and tastes pleasant it may be suitable to eat, but if it smells and tastes bad it could contain poisons. The snake appears to be tasting the air when it sticks out its tongue, but it is really collecting chemicals in the air, such as scents. It draws its tongue back into its mouth and pushes the tip into a pit in its nose where the chemicals are detected.

Growth and reproduction

Living things need food for energy to keep the body alive and for materials. They need the materials for growth and to repair parts of the body that have been damaged. Young animals, like the baby elephants in Figure 1.10, need food to grow healthily.

Figure 1.10 Elephants live in large family groups called herds, ruled by an elderly female called the matriarch.

Once the elephants are fully grown they need food to keep themselves in good health and to produce offspring. If the elephants did not produce offspring the herd would eventually disappear as the old elephants died. Reproduction is the process which keeps a plant or animal species in existence.

Excretion

When food and oxygen are used up in the body, waste products are made. These are poisonous, and if they build up inside the body they can kill it. To prevent this from happening the body has a way of getting rid of its harmful wastes. It is called excretion. Wastes are released in urine, sweat and the air that we breathe out. The waste product we release in our breath is carbon dioxide.

Testing for carbon dioxide

In exhaled breath

Exhaled air can be tested for carbon dioxide by passing it through limewater. If carbon dioxide is present it reacts with the calcium hydroxide dissolved in the water to produce insoluble calcium carbonate. This makes the water turn white or milky.

For discussion

How could you adapt the apparatus shown in Figure 1.11 to find out if

a) other animals produce carbon dioxide, and if

b) plants produce carbon dioxide?

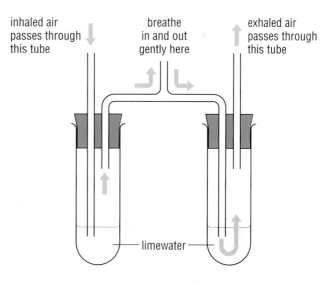

Figure 1.11 Testing inhaled and exhaled air for carbon dioxide.

In air around seeds

Carbon dioxide production can be used as an indication of respiration and a sign of life. Hydrogencarbonate indicator is a liquid that changes colour in the presence of carbon dioxide. It changes from an orange-red colour to yellow. The production of carbon dioxide by germinating pea seeds can be shown by setting up the apparatus shown in Figure 1.12.

For discussion

The apparatus shown in Figure 1.12 could be used to show that maggots release carbon dioxide. Should animals be used in experiments to show signs of life such as respiration?

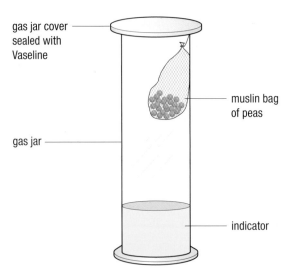

gas jar cover sealed with Vaseline

muslin bag of peas

gas jar

indicator

Figure 1.12   Investigating carbon dioxide production by germinating pea seeds.

◆ SUMMARY ◆

◆ There are seven characteristics of life – feeding, respiring, moving, growing, excreting, reproduction and irritability (*see page 10*).

◆ An animal with a skeleton on the outside of its body replaces it as it grows (*see page 11*).

◆ Green plants make food from oxygen and water (*see page 12*).

◆ Animals must obtain food from other living things (*see page 14*).

◆ Energy for life processes is released in respiration (*see page 14*).

◆ Muscles provide movement for all animals (*see page 15*).

◆ Sense organs are used to detect changes in the environment (*see page 15*).

◆ Food is needed for growth (*see page 16*).

◆ Plant and animal species stay in existence through reproduction (*see page 17*).

◆ Excretion is the release of harmful waste products (*see page 17*).

◆ Limewater is used to test for carbon dioxide (*see page 17*).

◆ Hydrogencarbonate indicator is used to test for carbon dioxide (*see page 18*).

End of chapter questions

The apparatus in Figure 1.13 is set up to show that seeds use up oxygen when they respire. The soda lime absorbs any carbon dioxide in the tube.

1   What happens to the coloured liquid in the tube as the seedlings respire?
2   Why does the volume of the gas around the seedlings change?
3   How would you use boiled seedlings to show that any change of gas was due to respiration?

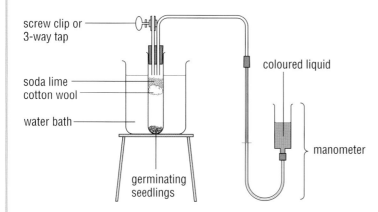

Figure 1.13

2

Major organ systems

Organs of a flowering plant

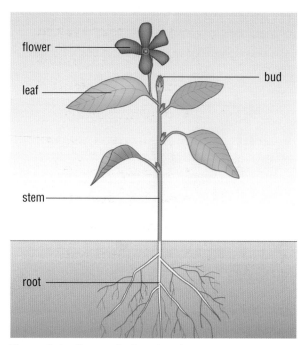

Figure 2.1 Organs of a flowering plant

1 Draw a table featuring the organs of a flowering plant and the tasks they perform.
2 How is the leaf dependent on the root and the stem?
3 Which life processes or tasks do you think are found in both plants and humans? Explain your answer.

There are five main organs in the body of a flowering plant. They are the root, stem, leaf, flower and bud. Each organ may be used for more than one task or life process.

1 The **root** anchors the plant and takes up water and minerals from the soil. The roots of some plants, such as the carrot, store food.
2 The **stem** transports water and food and supports the leaves and the flowers. Some plants, such as trees, store food in their stems.
3 The **leaf** produces food. In some plants, such as the onion, food is stored in the bases of the leaves. The swollen leaf bases make a bulb.
4 The **flower** contains the reproductive organs of the plant.
5 The **bud** contains tiny new branches, leaves and flowers ready to grow. These are delicate structures so the outside of the bud forms a protective covering to prevent them being damaged as they start to grow.

All the organs work together to keep the plant alive so that it can grow and produce offspring.

Organ systems of a human

Here are some of the major organ systems of the human body; the tasks they carry out are sometimes called life processes:

- **circulatory system**
- **respiratory system**
- **nervous system**
- **digestive system**
- **excretory system**
- **sensory system**
- **skeletal system**
- **muscle system**
- **endocrine system**

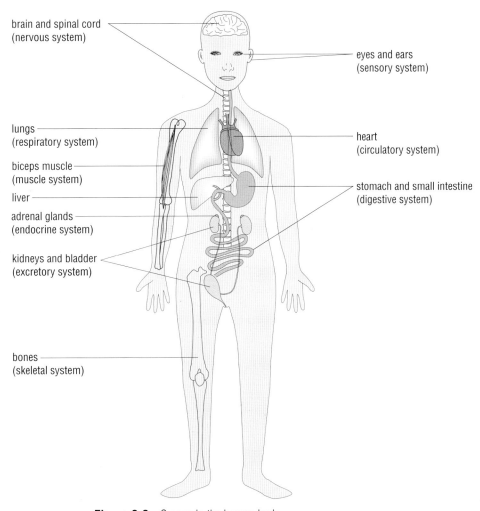

brain and spinal cord
(nervous system)

eyes and ears
(sensory system)

lungs
(respiratory system)

heart
(circulatory system)

biceps muscle
(muscle system)

liver

adrenal glands
(endocrine system)

stomach and small intestine
(digestive system)

kidneys and bladder
(excretory system)

bones
(skeletal system)

Figure 2.2 Organs in the human body.

A closer look at the circulatory system

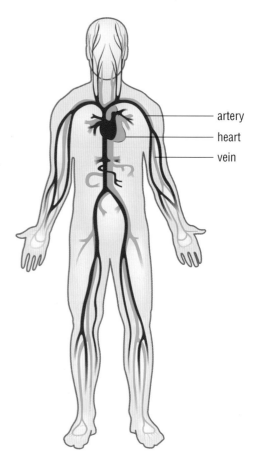

Figure 2.3 The heart and major arteries and veins.

The heart is located near the centre of the chest. It is made of muscle called cardiac muscle, which makes the heart beat. As the heart beats it pushes blood into the arteries and draws blood in from the veins. The beating of the heart makes the blood circulate around the body. The beating of the heart can be checked by taking the pulse. You can find your pulse by following these instructions.

1 Hold out your right hand with the palm up.
2 Put the thumb of your left hand under your wrist.
3 Let the first two fingers of your left hand rest on the top of your wrist.
4 Feel around on your wrist with these two fingers to find a throbbing artery. This is your pulse.
5 You can measure your pulse rate by counting how many times your pulse beats in a minute.

Figure 2.4 Measuring a pulse.

A closer look at the respiratory system

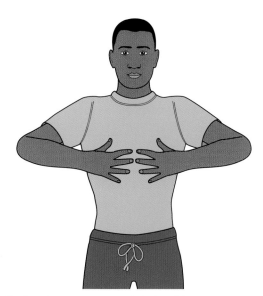

Figure 2.5 Feeling the movements made in breathing.

Breathing

Put your hands just below your ribs as you are reading these next few lines (Figure 2.5). As you read you should feel your hands moving in and out. They are being pushed by a muscle called the diaphragm. This helps in breathing as you will see in Chapter 8. If you stand up and place your hands on your ribs while breathing in and out you should feel your ribs move. The number of breaths you take in a certain time is called your rate of breathing. You take one breath when you breathe in and out once. The oxygen taken in during breathing is used to release energy from food.

If you have tried the breathing activity above you have already felt the action of part of your respiratory system – the ribs and diaphragm. They are the parts which move air in and out of the system or ventilate it.

Air enters in through the nose, passes down the back of the mouth and into the voice box and windpipe. You can feel your voice box and windpipe by placing your fingers on the front of your neck. They are hard because they are made of cartilage or gristle. This material helps to keep the airways open at all times.

The bottom of the windpipe divides into two tubes. Each one is called a bronchus. The two tubes together are called bronchi. The bronchi carry the air into the lungs. Here, some oxygen passes through the walls of the lungs into the blood. Carbon dioxide passes from the blood through the walls of the lungs into the air.

4 How does your pattern of breathing change when you exercise and then rest? Try a simple experiment to find the answer.

A closer look at the nervous system

The brain is enclosed in the skull and the spinal cord is enclosed in the spinal column (backbone). Nerves connect the brain to the eyes, ears, tongue, nose and skin on the head. Nerves also connect the spinal cord to the skin and to other organs in the body.

Messages travel through the nervous system as tiny electrical signals. The sense organs send signals to the spinal cord and the brain. If the brain decides that the body should move, it sends signals to the muscles.

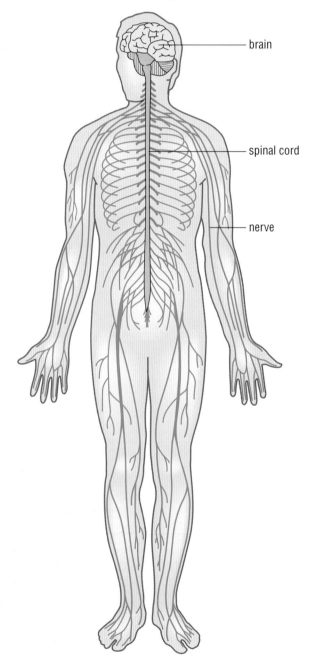

brain

spinal cord

nerve

Figure 2.6 The nervous system.

A closer look at the digestive system

The main part of the digestive system is a tube which runs through the body. It is called the alimentary canal (Figure 2.7). In an adult it is about 8 or 9 metres long. If you wind out a thread from a ball of wool until it is 9 metres long you will get an idea of the length of the alimentary canal. If you fold up the thread you will see that it can fit into a small space. The folding of the alimentary canal allows it to fit in the lower part of the body called the abdomen.

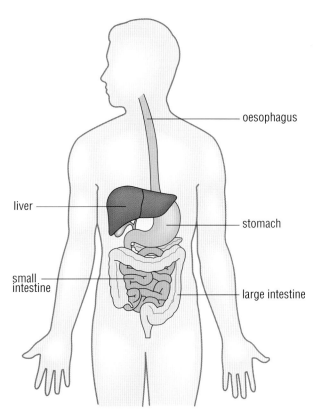

oesophagus

liver

stomach

small intestine

large intestine

Figure 2.7   The digestive system.

It takes between 24 and 48 hours for the food to travel along the alimentary canal, but journey times can vary quite widely. For example, a meal of boiled rice only stays in the stomach for up to 2 hours, while roast chicken may stay for up to 7 hours. Food begins its journey in the mouth, where it is broken up by the teeth and moistened by the saliva so that the small pieces can slide easily along. In the stomach the food is churned up into a creamy liquid called chyme, before it continues its journey into the intestines.

A closer look at the excretory system

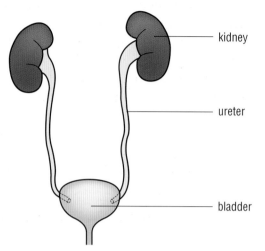

kidney

ureter

bladder

Figure 2.8 Organs involved in the excretion of urine. The urine from the kidneys is stored in the bladder before it is excreted.

The wastes produced by the body collect in the blood. As the blood passes through the kidneys a waste called urea is filtered from the blood with some water. This mixture of urea and water is called urine. As the blood passes through the skin on a hot day water and a little urea are taken from it and released onto the skin. The main purpose of this action is to cool the skin, although a little urea is also excreted. As the blood passes through the lungs carbon dioxide is removed and passed into the air, ready to be breathed out.

A closer look at the sensory system

The sensory system is made up of the sense organs – the eye, ear, nose, tongue and skin are the sense organs of sight, hearing, smell, taste and touch respectively. The function of this system is to provide information about

Figure 2.9 Yellow goatfish sensing each other's movements and moving together in a shoal.

5 Which organ system:
   a) transports materials around the body
   b) absorbs food into the blood
   c) detects changes in the environment
   d) co-ordinates activities
   e) takes in oxygen from the air
   f) supports the body
   g) removes waste from the blood
   h) moves bones?

6 Which organ system or systems are involved in:
   a) movement
   b) nutrition
   c) circulation?

7 What are the sense organs in the sensory system?

the surroundings of an animal. The information is sent in the form of electrical signals or messages along nerves in the nervous system to the brain.

Fish have a sense organ called the lateral line. A lateral line runs along the right and left sides of its body and it is sensitive to movements in the water. For example, when another fish swims by it causes movements in the water, and the lateral line detects them. From the information that the lateral line collects the fish can tell the distance of the other fish and the direction in which it is moving. This is important where fish live together in shoals and move quickly together to avoid predators.

A closer look at the skeletal system

The bones form the skeletal system of the body. In the human body there are 206 bones. Most of these provide support for the body and have joints between them to help the body move. Some bones, for example the bones in the skull, form a protective case around the body. The largest bone in the body is the femur (thigh bone), which provides support and movement, while the smallest bones in the body are in the ear and help the ear to detect sounds.

A closer look at the muscle system

Some people use weights to develop their skeletal muscle system, as Figure 2.10 shows. There are 656 muscles in the skeletal muscle system. They provide the

Figure 2.10 The muscle raising this weight is at the front of the upper arm and is called the biceps.

power to move the bones. Some on the front of the skull are attached to the skin and can move it to make expressions such as frowns or smiles. Muscles are capable of making themselves shorter. When skeletal muscles do this they pull on bones and move them. Muscles cannot make themselves longer again. They need another muscle close by to stretch them again. This second muscle does this by shortening itself. The muscle which stretches the biceps is called the triceps. The biceps is at the front of your upper arm and the triceps is behind it. If you raise your hand you can feel the biceps getting shorter and harder as it works. The triceps becomes longer and softer. When you lower your hand, your triceps becomes shorter and harder and the biceps becomes longer and softer. Muscles which work together in pairs like this are called antagonistic muscles.

There are two other kind of muscle – smooth muscle and cardiac muscle. Smooth muscle is found in other organ systems, such as the digestive system, where it moves the food along. The heart is made of cardiac muscle. Its movement pumps the blood around the body. The nervous system controls the movement of these two kinds of muscle automatically so you do not have to think about them.

8 What movements take place in the body that you do not have to think about?

A closer look at the endocrine system

The endocrine system is made up of glands which release chemicals called hormones into the blood. The adrenal gland is an example of an endocrine gland. It is found just above the kidney and releases (or secretes) a hormone called adrenaline. You feel the effect of adrenaline if you are asked to read aloud or act in front of a large audience, or take part in athletics. It makes your heart beat faster and directs more blood to your muscles.

9 What is the name of the hormone that makes your heart beat faster and directs more blood to your muscles?

10 You are walking across a road and hear a sound behind you. You turn and see that a car has swerved to avoid a donkey and is heading straight for you. What body systems work to get you out of the car's way? Why do you think these systems developed?

Hormones also control the way people grow and develop. The hormone insulin helps the body store a sugar which has been digested from food. A lack of this hormone in the body leads to a disease called diabetes. Diabetes can be controlled by taking extra insulin into the body.

Exercise

Regular exercise makes many of the organ systems become more efficient. It also uses up energy and helps to prevent large amounts of fat building up in the body.

Exercise can increase your fitness in three ways: it can improve your strength, make your body more flexible and less likely to suffer from sprains, and it can increase your endurance, which is your ability to exercise steadily for long periods without resting. Different activities require different levels of fitness. Table 2.1 shows these levels for different sporting activities. By studying the table you can work out which activities you could do to develop one or more of the three components of fitness.

11 Which activities demand great flexibility?

12 Which activity is the least demanding?

13 Which activities are the most demanding?

14 How do the demands of soccer and long distance running compare?

15 Which activity would you choose from the table? What are its strengths and weaknesses?

16 Many people claim that they do not have time to exercise. How would you motivate such people to take some form of exercise? Which activities might suit them best?

Table 2.1

Activity	Strength	Flexibility	Endurance
Basketball	✔✔	✔✔	✔✔✔
Dancing	✔✔	✔✔✔	✔✔
Golf	✔✔	✔✔	✔✔
Long distance running	✔✔✔	✔✔	✔✔✔
Soccer	✔✔	✔✔	✔✔✔
Squash	✔✔✔	✔✔✔	✔✔✔
Swimming	✔✔✔	✔✔	✔✔✔
Tennis	✔✔✔	✔✔✔	✔✔✔
Walking	✔	✔	✔✔

Figure 2.11

◆ SUMMARY ◆

- ◆ The five main organs of the flowering plant are the root, stem, leaf, flower and bud (*see page 20*).
- ◆ Some of the major organ systems of the human body are the circulatory system, the respiratory system, the nervous system, the digestive system, the excretory system, the sensory system, the skeletal system, the muscle system and the endocrine system (*see page 21*).
- ◆ The beating of the heart can be checked by taking the pulse (*see page 22*).
- ◆ The movement of the ribs and diaphragm ventilate the respiratory system (*see page 23*).
- ◆ The nervous system comprises the brain, spinal cord and nerves. The main part of the digestive system is a tube which runs through the body (*see pages 24 and 25*).
- ◆ Excretion is the removal of wastes that are produced by the body (*see page 26*).
- ◆ The sensory system is made up of the sense organs - the eye, ear, nose, tongue and skin (*see page 26*).
- ◆ The bones make up the skeletal system (*see page 27*).
- ◆ There are three types of muscle in the human body (*see pages 27–28*).
- ◆ The endocrine system is made up of glands which release hormones into the blood (*see page 28*).
- ◆ Regular exercise makes the organ systems more efficient (*see page 28*).
- ◆ Different activities for exercise need different levels of fitness (*see page 29*).

End of chapter questions

1 Name three organs of a flowering plant which may be used to store food.
2 What action would you take to check your heartbeat?
3 Name four structures in your body that air passes through as it moves to the lungs.
4 In which organ system of the human body is the
   a) adrenal gland
   b) bladder
   c) liver?
5 Regular exercise prevents the build up of which substance in the body?

3 Cells

You are probably aware that there are large numbers of different living things. Just think of the animals that you may see at a zoo, or the different plants that you may see in a park. You may also be aware that even among the same kind of living things there is variety. Just think of how you recognise different people by their own characteristic features. When scientists are looking at the features of living things they make careful observations and accurate records of what they see.

Making observations

1 How are the leaves arranged in plant A and plant B in Figure 3.1?

2 How are the flowers arranged in A and B?

When you make observations you look closely and with a purpose. For example, you may *look* at a plant and just see its flowers and leaves, but if you *observed* a plant you could study it to find out how the leaves and flowers are arranged on the stem. Leaves can be arranged in many ways; for example, they may grow alternately along a stem or they may be arranged in pairs. Flowers may be arranged singly or in columns.

B St John's wort

A Rosebay willow herb

Figure 3.1 The leaves and flowers in two plants.

Drawing specimens

Explorers of the 17th and 18th Centuries collected specimens of the plants and animals they found and brought them back to the scientists in Europe for further study. Many of the living things died during the journey, and by the time they arrived their remains were decayed and of little use to the scientists. Even when the specimens were kept in a preservative their colours would be lost or some other feature would change. To solve the problem of showing how these living things appeared in their habitats, artists accompanied the explorers and drew pictures of the plants and animals that were discovered. The scientists back in Europe could then use both the specimens and the pictures to help them study and classify the new living things that were being discovered.

1 Why were artists taken on explorations in the 17th and 18th Centuries?
2 Why do you think artists are used much less in expeditions today?
3 Why might an organism be drawn ×5? Give an example. Why might another organism be drawn $\times\frac{1}{2}$? Give an example.
4 What is the true size of the living things in these drawings?

Figure A   17th Century biological drawing.

Biological drawings of specimens are still made today. The size of the specimen is usually indicated in one of two ways. A line may be drawn next to the picture to indicate the length of the specimen, or the drawing may have ×5 or $\times\frac{1}{2}$ next to it. The × symbol means times larger or smaller; the number gives an indication of the size. For example, ×5 means the drawing is five times larger than the specimen, and $\times\frac{1}{2}$ means the drawing is half the size of the specimen.

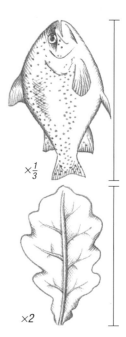

Figure B   A leaf and a fish.

The microscope

A microscope is used for looking at specimens very closely. Most laboratory microscopes give a magnification up to about 200 times but some can give a magnification of over 1000 times. The microscope must also provide a clear view, and this is achieved by controlling the amount of light shining onto the specimen.

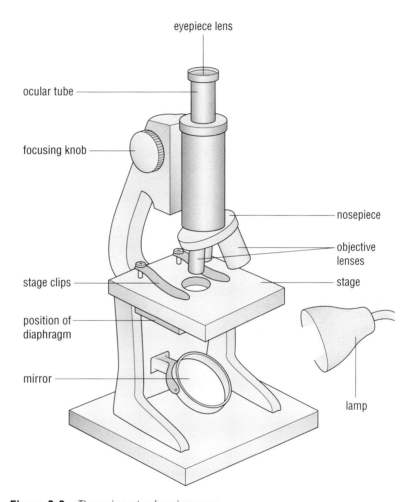

Figure 3.2 The main parts of a microscope.

Light is collected by a mirror at the base of the microscope. The mirror is held in special joints that allow it to move in any direction. The light comes from a lamp or from a sunless sky. It must never be collected directly from the Sun as this can cause severe eye damage and blindness. Some microscopes have a built-in lamp instead of a mirror. The light either shines directly through a hole in the stage onto the specimen or it passes through a hole in a diaphragm. The

3 What is a microscope used for?

4 What advice would you give someone about how to collect light to shine into a microscope?

5 What magnification would you get by using an eyepiece of ×5 magnification with an objective lens of ×10 magnification?

6 If you had a microscope with ×5 and ×10 eyepieces and objective lens of ×10, 15 and 20, what powers of magnification could your microscope provide?

7 How would you advise someone to use the three objective lenses on the nosepiece?

8 Why should you not look down the microscope all the time as you try to focus the specimen?

9 Look at the picture of the microscope on page 33 and describe the path taken by light from a lamp near the microscope to the eye.

diaphragm allows the amount of light reaching the specimen to be controlled by increasing or decreasing the size of the hole. The light shining through a specimen is called transmitted light.

Above the specimen is the ocular tube. This has an eyepiece lens at the top and one or more objective lenses at the bottom. The magnification of the two lenses is written on them. An eyepiece lens may give a magnification of ×5 or ×10. An objective lens may give a magnification of ×10, ×15 or ×20. The magnification provided by both the eyepiece lens and the objective lens is found by multiplying their magnifying powers together. Most microscopes have three objective lenses on a nosepiece at the bottom of the ocular tube. The nosepiece can be rotated to bring each objective lens under the ocular tube in turn. An investigation with the microscope always starts by using the lowest power objective lens then working up to the highest power objective lens if it is required.

A specimen for viewing under the microscope must be put on a glass slide. The slide is put on the stage and held in place by the stage clips. The slide should be positioned so that the specimen is in the centre of the hole in the stage.

The view of the specimen is brought into focus by turning the focusing knob on the side of the microscope. This may raise or lower the ocular tube or it may raise or lower the stage on which the slide of the specimen is held. In either case you should watch from the side of the microscope as you turn the knob to bring the objective lens and specimen close together. If you looked down the ocular tube as you did this you might crash the objective lens into the specimen, which could damage both the lens and the specimen. When the objective lens and the specimen are close together, but not touching, look down the eyepiece and turn the focusing knob so that the objective lens and specimen move apart. If you do this slowly, the blurred image will become clear.

Finding the size of microscopic specimens

The disc of light you see when you look down a microscope is called the field of view. You can estimate the size of the specimens you see under the microscope if you know the size of the field of view. A simple way to find the size of the field of view is to put a piece of

10 A field of view was found to be 2000 µm in diameter. A soil particle reached one quarter of the way across it. How long would you estimate the length of the particle to be?

11 The fields of view of three lenses were measured. A was 100 µm, B was 3000 µm and C was 500 µm. Which was the most powerful lens and which was the least powerful lens?

12 Why does the field of view decrease as the power of the objective lens increases?

graph paper on a slide and examine it using the low power objective lens. The squares on the graph should be 1 mm across. Microscopic measurements are not made in millimetres, they are measured in micrometres. 1 mm = 1000 micrometres (written as 1000 µm).

If the field of view is two squares across it has a diameter of 2000 µm. If you remove the slide with the graph paper and replace it with a slide with some soil particles, you could estimate the size of a soil particle by judging how far it crosses the field of view.

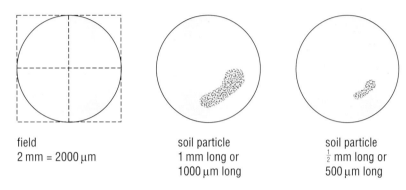

field
2 mm = 2000 µm

soil particle
1 mm long or
1000 µm long

soil particle
$\frac{1}{2}$ mm long or
500 µm long

Figure 3.3 A soil particle under the microscope.

If the soil particle comes halfway across the field of view it is 1000 µm long. There is a relationship between the power of an objective lens and its field of view. As the power of the objective lens increases, the size of its field of view decreases.

From organs to cells

Marie F. X. Bichat (1771–1802) was a French doctor who did many post mortem examinations. In the last year of his life he carried out 600. He cut up the bodies of dead people to find out how they had died. From this he discovered that organs were made of layers of materials. He called these layers 'tissues' and identified 21 different kinds. For a while scientists thought that tissues were made of simple non-living materials.

In 1665, long before Bichat was born, an English scientist named Robert Hooke (1635–1703) used a microscope to investigate the structure of a very thin sheet of cork. He discovered that it had tiny compartments in it. He thought of them as rooms and called them 'cells', after the small rooms in monasteries where monks worked and meditated.

Bichat did not examine the tissues he had found under a microscope because most of those made at that time did not produce very clear images. When better microscopes were made, scientists investigated pieces of plants and found that, like cork, they also had a cell structure. The cells in

1 Where did Bichat get his ideas that organs were made from tissues?

2 Who first described 'cells' and where did the idea for the word come from?

3 Who named the nucleus and what does it mean?

(continued)

Hooke's piece of cork had been empty but other plant cells were found to contain structures.

A Scottish scientist called Robert Brown (1773–1858) studied plant cells and noticed that each one had a dark spot inside it. In 1831 he named the spot the 'nucleus' which means 'little nut'.

Matthias Schleiden (1804–1881) was a German scientist who studied the parts of many plants. In 1838 he put forward a theory that all plants were made of cells. A year later Theodor Schwann, another German scientist, stated that animals were also made of cells.

The ideas of Schleiden and Schwann became known as the Cell Theory. It led other scientists to make more discoveries about cells and to show that tissues are made up of groups of similar cells.

4 What instrument was essential for the study of cells?

5 How could the Cell Theory have been developed sooner?

6 Arrange these parts of a body in order of size starting with the largest: cell, organ, tissue, organ system.

Cells

There are ten times more cells in your body than there are people on the Earth. If you stay in the water in a swimming pool for a long time you may notice sometimes that when you dry yourself part of your skin flakes off. These flakes are made of dead skin cells. You are losing skin cells all the time but in a much smaller way. As your clothes rub against your skin they pull off tiny flakes which pass into the air and settle in the dust. A small part of the dirt that cleaners sweep up at the end of a school day comes from the skin that the pupils have left behind.

Figure 3.4 shows a section of human skin that has been stained and photographed down a microscope using a high power objective lens. When unstained, the different parts of the cells are colourless and are difficult to distinguish. In the 1870s it was discovered that dyes could be made from coal tar which would stain different

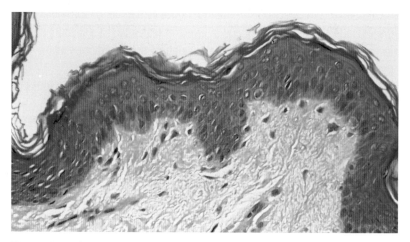

Figure 3.4 Section of human skin. Cells can be seen flaking off the surface.

13 Why are most specimens of cells stained before they are examined under the microscope?

14 Imagine that you are looking down a microscope at a slide labelled 'Cells'. You can see a coloured substance with dots in it and lines that divide the substance into rectangular shapes. Inside the rectangular shapes, what are:
 a) the dots
 b) the lines
 c) the coloured substance?

parts of the cell. Cell biologists found they could stain the nucleus and other parts of the cell different colours to see them more easily.

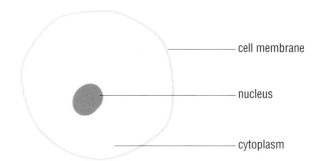

Figure 3.5 A typical animal cell.

Basic parts of a cell

Nucleus

This is the control centre of the cell. It contains the genetic material called DNA (its full name is deoxyribonucleic acid). The DNA molecule is a long chain of smaller molecules. They occur in different combinations along the DNA molecule. The combinations of molecules provide instructions for the cell to make chemicals to keep it alive or to build its cell parts. When a cell divides the DNA divides too, so that the nucleus of each new cell receives all the instructions to keep the new cell alive and enable it to grow.

Cytoplasm

This is a watery jelly which fills most of each animal cell. It can move around inside the cell. The cytoplasm may contain stored food in the form of grains. Most of the chemical reactions that keep the cell alive take place in the cytoplasm.

Cell membrane

This covers the outside of the cell. It has tiny holes in it called pores that control the movement of chemicals in or out of the cell. Dissolved substances such as food, oxygen and carbon dioxide can pass through the cell membrane. Some harmful chemicals are stopped from entering the cell by the membrane.

15 How does the cell membrane protect the cell?

16 If there are about 6000 million people on the Earth, how many cells have you got in your body?

Parts found only in plant cells

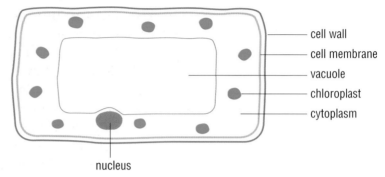

Figure 3.6 A typical plant cell.

Cell wall

This is found outside the membrane of a plant cell. It is made of cellulose, which is a tough material that gives support to the cell.

Chloroplasts

These are found in the cytoplasm of many plant cells. They contain a green pigment called chlorophyll which traps a small amount of the energy in sunlight. This energy is used by the plant to make food in a process called photosynthesis (see Chapter 11). Chloroplasts are found in many leaf cells and in the stem cells of some plants.

Large vacuole

This large space in the cytoplasm of a plant cell is filled with a liquid called cell sap which contains dissolved sugars and salts. When the vacuole is full of cell sap the liquid pushes outwards on the cell wall and gives it support. If the plant is short of water, the support is lost and the plant wilts.

Some animal cells and Protoctista have vacuoles but they are much smaller than those found in plant cells.

Adaptation in cells

The word adaptation means the change of an existing design for a particular task (see also page 194). The basic designs of animal and plant cells were shown in the last section, but many cells are adapted, which allows them to perform a more specific task. Here are some common examples of the different types of animal and plant cells.

17 Name two things that give support to a plant cell.

18 Would you expect to find chloroplasts in a root cell? Explain your answer.

19 Why do plants wilt if they are not watered regularly?

Red blood cells

Red blood cells are disc-shaped but their centres dip inwards. The structure is called a biconcave disc. Red cells only have a nucleus when they are growing. They lose it so that they can become packed with haemoglobin when they are fully grown. Haemoglobin combines with oxygen in the lungs to form oxyhaemoglobin. The red blood cells carry this substance to parts of the body where oxygen is needed. When the cells reach their destination, they release the oxygen. Haemoglobin forms again ready for another trip to the lungs.

Figure 3.7 Red blood cell.

White blood cells

These have an irregular shape, in fact they keep changing shape as the cytoplasm flows about inside them. One kind of white cell, a lymphocyte, produces antibodies, which attack harmful microorganisms in the blood such as bacteria. A second kind of white cell, a phagocyte, eats the harmful microorgansims.

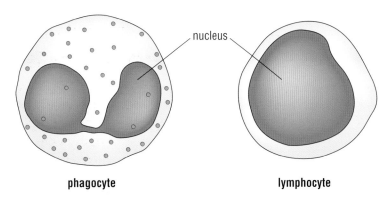

nucleus

phagocyte

lymphocyte

Figure 3.8 White blood cells.

Smooth muscle cells

Once you swallow food it is moved through your body by smooth muscle cells. These cells are spindle-shaped and lie together forming muscular tissue around the wall of the oesophagus, stomach and intestines. Muscle cells can only use their energy to contract or get shorter; they need other muscles to stretch them back to their original lengths. For this reason smooth muscle cells are arranged in layers at right angles to each other. When the cells in one layer contract they squeeze food through your body. When the cells in the next layer contract they stretch the muscles in the first layer so they can contract again and move more food.

20 What happens to the smooth muscle cells in the second layer in Figure 3.9 when the muscle cells in the first layer are contracting?

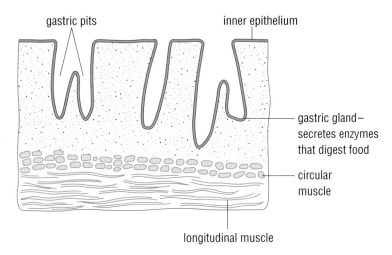

Figure 3.9 The stomach wall has layers of muscular tissue that churn up food and move it through the stomach. Gland tissue above the muscular tissue helps to digest some of the food in the stomach.

Nerve cells

Nerves are made from nerve cells or neurones, which have long thread-like extensions. These nerve cells are connected to other nerve cells in the spinal cord. The nerve cells in the spinal cord are then connected to nerve cells in the brain.

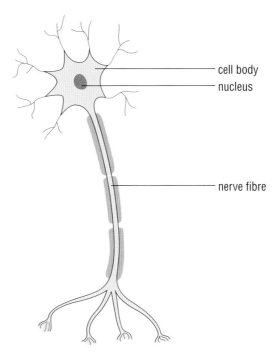

Figure 3.10 Nerve cell.

Ciliated epithelial cells

Cells that line the surface of structures are called epithelial cells. Cilia are microscopic hair-like extensions of the cytoplasm. If cells have one surface covered in cilia they are described as ciliated. Ciliated epithelial cells line the throat. Air entering the throat contains dust that becomes trapped in the mucus of the throat lining. The cilia wave to and fro and carry the dust trapped in the mucus away from the lungs.

21 In what ways are red and white blood cells different?

22 Smoking damages the cilia lining the breathing tubes. What effect might this have on breathing?

23 Why are there different kinds of cells?

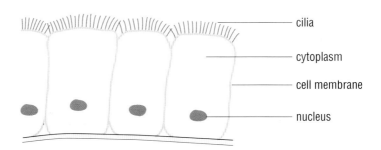

Figure 3.11 Ciliated epithelial cells.

Root hair cells

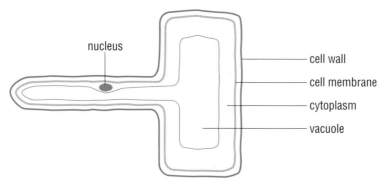

Figure 3.12 A root hair cell.

These grow a short distance behind the root tip. The cells have long thin extensions that allow them to grow easily between the soil particles. The shape of these extensions gives the root hair cells a large surface area through which water can be taken up from the soil.

24 What changes have taken place in the basic plant cell to produce a root hair cell?

25 How is a palisade cell different from a root hair cell? Explain these differences.

26 Why would it be a problem if root hair cell extensions were short and stubby?

Palisade cells

These plant cells have a shape that allows them to pack closely together in the upper part of a leaf, near the light. They have large numbers of chloroplasts in them to trap as much light energy as possible.

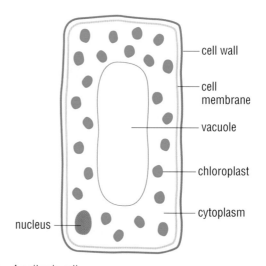

Figure 3.13 A palisade cell.

There are many kinds of living thing which have bodies made from just one cell. They are microbes – the most numerous living things on the planet.

From cells to organ systems

The cells in the body of a living thing are arranged into groups. The cells in a group are all of the same kind and perform a special task in the life of the organism. For example, the cells near the surface of your skin (see Figure 3.4 page 36) are broad and flat and provide a protective covering like the flags in a pavement. The group of similar cells which perform a task like this is called a tissue. Tissues of different cells join together to also perform a task in the life of an organism. For example, Figure 3.9 (page 40) shows the stomach wall. It is made up from four tissues: smooth muscle tissue, a tissue of cells forming a cover inside the stomach, a tissue of cells making the glands which produce digestive juices, and a tissue of supporting cells to separate the glands and hold them above the muscles.

These four tissues work together to digest protein food in the stomach (see page 108). Organs do not work on their own in a body. Their work is related to the work of other organs. For example, the stomach digests protein but other organs in the body help in the digestion of food. These organs are connected together and form a larger structure called a system. The stomach is part of the digestive system. When studying the bodies of living things it is important to keep in mind how the different parts are related. The way that cells are related to organ systems is through the following links:

cells → tissues → organs → organ systems

♦ SUMMARY ♦

♦ You make observations by looking closely with a purpose (*see page 31*).
♦ The microscope is used to observe very small living things or the cells of larger living things (*see page 33*).
♦ There are special techniques for finding the size of small objects with a microscope (*see page 34*).
♦ The bodies of plants and animals are made of cells. The basic parts of the cell are the nucleus, cytoplasm and cell membrane (*see page 37*).
♦ In a plant cell there is a cellulose cell wall and a vacuole (*see page 38*).
♦ Cells have different forms for different functions. They are adapted to do specific tasks in the body and life of the organism (*see page 38*).
♦ Cells are grouped together into tissues. Tissues are grouped together to make organs (*see pages 42–43*).
♦ A number of organs which work together is called an organ system (*see page 43*).

End of chapter question

1 a) Which part of a cell **i)** has pores that control movement of chemicals, **ii)** is made from cellulose, **iii)** contains DNA, **iv)** contains chlorophyll, **v)** is made from watery jelly, **vi)** contains cell sap?
b) Which of the above parts are found only in plant cells?

4 Classification and variation

Classifying living things

Living things are put into groups so that they can be studied more easily. The largest groups are called kingdoms. Scientists have now named five kingdoms. Each kingdom contains a large number of living things that all have a few major features in common. Table 4.1 shows the features that are used to place living things in either the plant or animal kingdom.

Table 4.1 The features of living things in the plant and animal kingdoms.

Plant kingdom	Animal kingdom
Make their own food from air, water, sunlight and chemicals in the soil	Cannot make their own food. Eat plants and animals
Body contains cellulose for support	Body does not contain cellulose
Have the green pigment chlorophyll	Do not have chlorophyll
Stay in one place	Move about

There are five kingdoms of living things. They are the animal kingdom (see below), the plant kingdom (see page 50), the fungi kingdom (see page 50), the Monera kingdom which include bacteria, and a kingdom known as Protoctista.

Dividing up a kingdom

The way that the animal kingdom is divided up into subgroups is described on the following pages. A similar way of subgrouping is used to divide up the other kingdoms.

Subgroups of the animal kingdom

The subgroups of the animal kingdom can be put into two groups called the invertebrates and the vertebrates. Invertebrates do not have an inside skeleton of cartilage or

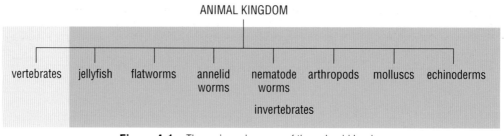

Figure 4.1 The major subgroups of the animal kingdom.

bone. Vertebrates do have an inside skeleton of cartilage or bone. These two groups can be divided further.

Groups of invertebrates

The main subgroups in the invertebrate group are the jellyfish, flatworms, annelid worms, nematode worms, arthropods, molluscs and echinoderms.

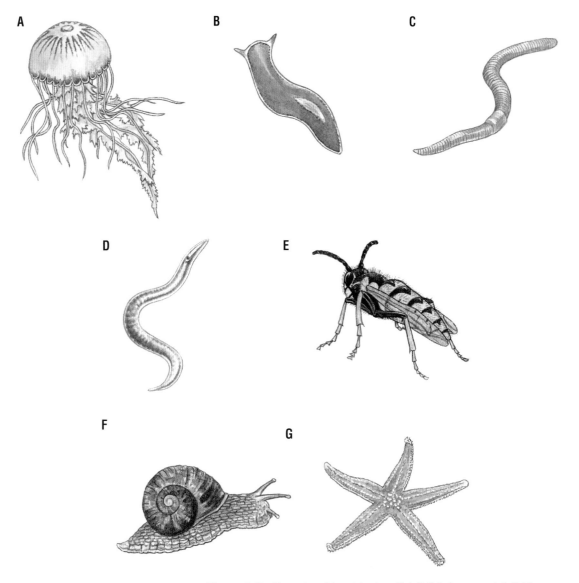

1 How is an earthworm different from a wasp? How is it similar to a wasp?

Figure 4.2 Examples of invertebrates. A) jellyfish (compass jellyfish), B) flatworm (pond flatworm), C) annelid worm (earthworm), D) nematode worm (roundworm), E) arthropod (wasp), F) mollusc (snail) and G) echinoderm (starfish).

Annelids

Annelids have long, thin, soft bodies divided into segments or rings.

Figure 4.3 An earthworm crawling through soil.

Nematodes

Nematodes have thin, cylindrical bodies that are not divided into segments.

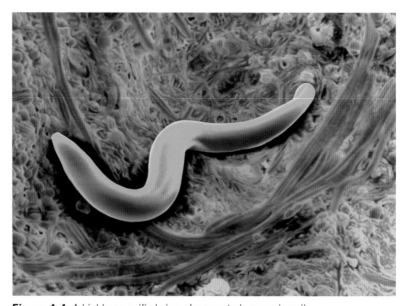

Figure 4.4 A highly-magnified view of a nematode worm in soil.

Arthropods

The name arthropod means 'jointed leg'. All arthropods have a skeleton on the outside of their body and jointed legs.

There are four major classes of arthropods. Myriapods have one pair of antennae and long cylindrical or flat bodies with many legs. The centipedes and millipedes are in this group (see page 55). Crustaceans, like the lobster and woodlouse, have two pairs of antennae. Insects have one pair of antennae, three pairs of legs and up to two pairs of wings. Arachnids do not have antennae or wings but have four pairs of legs. Spiders, mites, ticks and scorpions belong to this group.

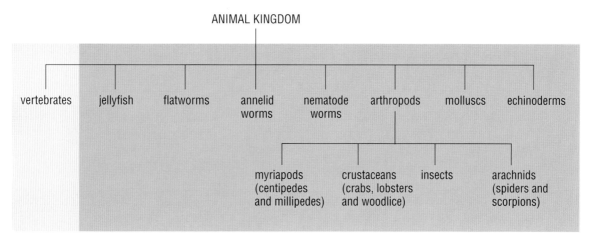

Figure 4.5 The classes of arthropods in the animal kingdom.

Figure 4.6 A giant millipede on the floor of a rainforest.

Figure 4.7 A lobster walking along the seabed.

Figure 4.8 A black widow spider – one of the most venomous spiders in the world.

Figure 4.9 The Monarch butterfly is found all over the world in tropical and sub-tropical areas.

Molluscs

The mollusc group gets its name from the Latin word *mollis*, which means soft. This refers to the soft bodies of the animals. Most molluscs have a shell to protect their body. A snail has a coiled shell from which it pushes out its head and fleshy 'foot' when it wishes to move and feed. The slug also has a small shell, but it is under the saddle-like structure (called the mantle) on its back, and does not provide protection.

Figure 4.10 An octopus on a coral reef. An octopus is a mollusc with tentacles.

Groups of vertebrates

The vertebrate group includes fish, amphibians, reptiles, birds and mammals.

Table 4.2 The features of five of the vertebrate classes.

Bony fish	Amphibians	Reptiles	Birds	Mammals
Scales, fins Eggs laid in water	Smooth skin Eggs laid in water	Scales. Soft-shelled eggs laid on land	Feathers Hard-shelled eggs	Hair Suckle young with milk

Figure 4.11 The duck-billed platypus is an egg-laying mammal which lives in Australia.

Figure 4.12 The kiwi is a flightless bird which lives in New Zealand.

Other kingdoms of living things

The plant kingdom

There are four groups in the plant kingdom including conifers and flowering plants. The conifers are large evergreen trees. They make seeds that develop in cones. The flowering plant group has both small and large species (see Chapter 10). Some have woody stems like the fig, and grow into trees.

Figure 4.13 The fig plant has a woody stem.

The fungi kingdom

Fungi cells have walls made of chitin, unlike plant cells, which have walls made of cellulose. Fungi cannot photosynthesise, so most kinds of fungi produce threads called hyphae, and use these to feed on dead plants and animals. Moulds, mushrooms and toadstools are familiar fungi that feed in this way.

The athlete's foot fungus is a parasite which feeds on damp skin between the toes. Yeasts are tiny fungi which can be seen only by using a microscope. They feed on the sugar that forms on the surfaces of fruits and in the nectar of flowers.

Fungi reproduce by making spores. Mushrooms and toadstools produce umbrella-shaped fruiting bodies which rise above the round to help the spores spread out on air currents.

Figure 4.14 Fairy-ring mushroom. The feeding threads (hyphae) form a disc in the soil. At the edges of the disc, fruiting bodies form to release spores.

Viruses

Viruses do not have a cell structure. They can be stored like mineral specimens for many years without changing. During this time they do not feed, respire or excrete. When they are placed on living tissues they enter the living cells and reproduce. They destroy the cells in the process and may cause disease.

What is a species?

A species is a group of animals that have a very large number of similarities and the males and females breed together to produce offspring that can also breed. The males and females of different species do not normally breed together, but when they do they produce offspring that are usually sterile (cannot breed). For example, a male donkey and a female horse produce a sterile mule.

A species has special features which allow it to survive in a particular environment. For example, a polar bear has features which allow it to survive in the cold environment of the Arctic. Polar bears are predators and need to be able to approach their prey unseen. The white fur camouflages them in the white Arctic landscape and makes them difficult for prey to see. The fur is very thick and it forms an insulation

For discussion
Are viruses living things? Explain your answer.

For discussion
What features do you think a polar bear has that allows it to survive in a cold environment?

Should we care if the polar bear becomes extinct?

blanket over the bear's body to keep in its body heat. The bear also stores up layers of fat for insulation. Much of the polar bear's habitat is covered in ice. Hairs on the feet help the bear to grip the ice as it stalks and chases its prey. However, if the Arctic conditions become warmer the polar bear does not have the features to help it cope with the change, and it will die out and become extinct.

Figure 4.15 A polar bear in its natural habitat.

Keys

The way in which living things are divided up into groups can be used to identify them (see page 53).

Spider key

On each 'leg' of the spider is a feature that is possessed by the living thing below it. An example is shown in Figure 4.16. A spider key is read by starting at the top in the centre and reading the features down the legs until the specimen is identified.

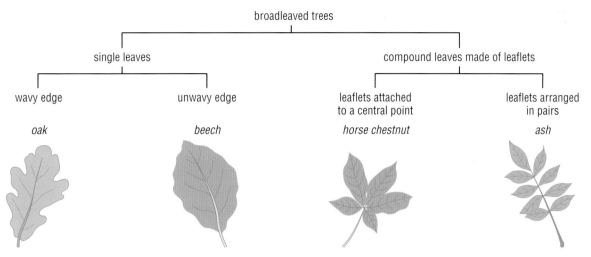

Figure 4.16   Spider key of leaves from broadleaved trees.

2   Make a spider key for the four animals in Figure 4.17. Look carefully at the animals. Choose a feature they have all got in common to start at the top of the key.

Figure 4.17   Molluscs and annelid worms.

Numbered key

You work through a numbered key by reading each pair of statements and matching the description of one of them to the features you see on the specimen you are trying to identify. At the end of each statement there is an instruction to move to another pair of statements or to the name of a living thing. Here is a simple numbered key. It can be used to identify molluscs that live in freshwater habitats such as rivers, lakes and ponds.

1 a) Single shell .... see 2
b) Two shells .... see 6
2 a) Snail with a plate that closes the shell mouth .... *Bithynia*
b) Snail without a plate that closes the shell mouth .... see 3
3 a) Snail without a twisted shell .... Freshwater
.... limpet
b) Snail with a twisted shell..................... see 4
4 a) Shell in a coil .... Ramshorn
.... snail
b) Shell without a coil.............................. see 5
5 a) Snail with triangular tentacles............ Pond snail
b) Snail with long, thin tentacles............. Bladder snail
6 a) Animal has threads attaching it to a surface .... Zebra mussel
b) Animal does not have threads attaching it to a surface...................... see 7
7 a) Shell larger than 25 mm .... Freshwater
.... mussel
b) Shell smaller than 25 mm .... Pea mussel

3 Identify the molluscs A–F in Figure 4.18 using the numbered key on page 53. In each case write down the number of each statement you used to make the identification.

4 Why should another feature in addition to size be added to the statements in part 7 of the key?

A

B

C

D

E

F

Figure 4.18 Some freshwater molluscs.

When using a numbered key write down the numbers of the statements you followed to identify your specimen. For example, specimen A is identified by following statements **1a**, **2b**, **3a**. It is a freshwater limpet.

5 Make up a numbered key to identify the arthropods in Figure 4.19. Begin by separating the butterfly, which has six legs, from the others.

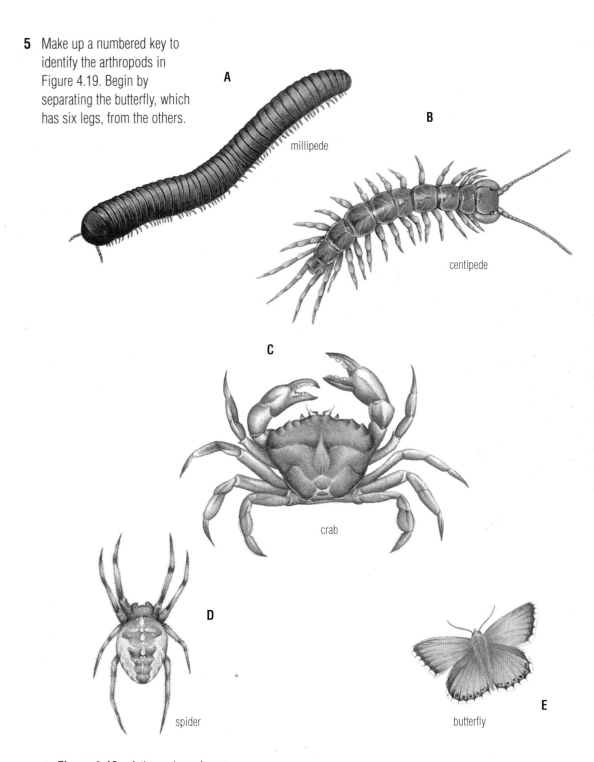

A millipede

B centipede

C crab

D spider

E butterfly

Figure 4.19 Arthropod specimens.

6 Look at the parts of the insect's body in Figure 4.20a. Then look at how the parts vary among the six insect specimens in b. Invent a key to identify them.

7 Look at the numbered key for freshwater molluscs and the spider key for the leaves (both on page 53) and answer the following questions.

   a) Which key identifies the larger number of living things?

   b) If both keys featured the same number of living things, which key would need the larger amount of space?

   c) What is an advantage of the numbered key?

   d) What is an advantage of a spider key?

   e) Which is the better one to use in a poster? Explain.

   f) Which is the better one to use in a pocket book for field work? Explain.

a)

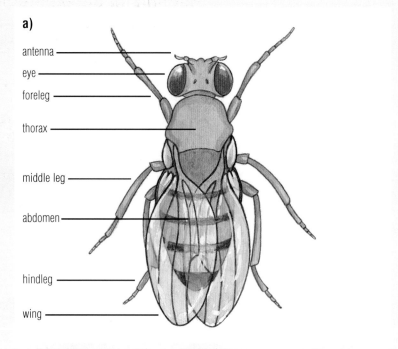

b)

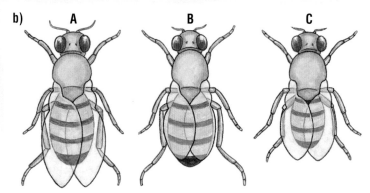

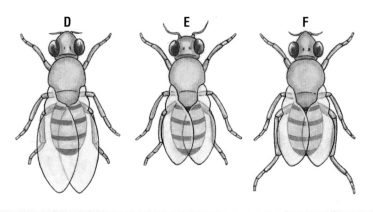

Figure 4.20 Variation in flies.

Animals in the laboratory

Small animals such as invertebrates can be studied in the laboratory or animal house by setting up a habitat that is similar to their own.

Snails

Snails can be kept in an aquarium tank. The floor of the tank should be covered with a mixture of damp soil and peat. Large stones may be placed in the mixture for the snails to climb on and hide under.

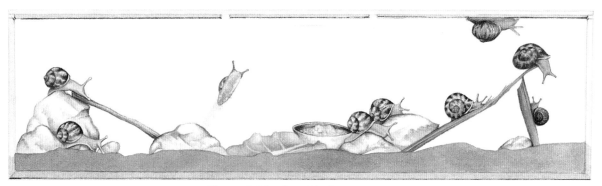

Figure 4.21 A snail tank.

Woodlice

Woodlice can also be kept in an aquarium tank if the floor is covered with soil and a layer of damp moss and pieces of bark.

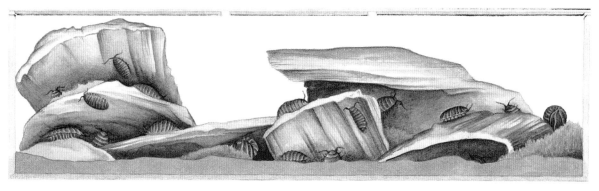

Figure 4.22 A woodlouse tank.

8 The woodlice were also observed in damp conditions but not in dry ones. How would you set up the shallow tray to test this observation?

Investigating behaviour

Experiments can be devised to investigate the way the animals behave after observing them in the tanks. For example, it may be noticed that the woodlice are found under the bark in the daytime. This observation may lead to the idea that woodlice do not like the light. This idea can be tested by putting the woodlice in a shallow tray,

9 When checking the behaviour of the woodlice in their habitat some were found under a log one day and under a stone about a metre away the next day. When do you think they moved? Explain your answer.

part of which is uncovered and in the light and part of which is covered and in the dark. The woodlice should be placed in the centre of the tray and left for a few minutes before recording where they have settled to rest.

Variation

Variation between species

Many living things have certain features in common. For example a cat, a monkey and a rabbit have ears and a tail. However, these features vary from one kind of animal to the next. In the species shown in the photographs below, the external parts of the ears of the rabbit are longer than the ears of the cat. The external parts of the monkey's ears are on the side of its head while the other two animals have them on the top. The cat and the monkey have long tails but the monkey's tail is prehensile, which means it can wrap it around a branch for support while it hangs from a tree to collect fruit. (Only monkeys that come from South America have prehensile tails.) A rabbit's tail is much shorter than the cat's tail and the monkey's tail. These variations in features are used to separate living things into groups and form a classification system which is used worldwide.

Figure 4.23   A cat, a rabbit and a South American monkey.

Variation within a species

The individuals in a species are not identical. Each one differs from all the others in many small ways. For example, one person may have dark hair, blue eyes and ears with lobes while another person may have fair hair, brown eyes and ears without lobes. Another person may have different combinations of these features.

There are two kinds of variation that occur in a species. They are continuous variation and discontinuous variation.

Continuous variation

A feature that shows continuous variation may vary in only a small amount from one individual to the next, but when the variations of a number of individuals are compared they form a wide range. Examples include the range of values seen in different heights or body masses.

Discontinuous variation

A feature that shows discontinuous variation shows a small number of distinct conditions, such as being male or female and having ear lobes or no ear lobes. There is not a range of stages between the two as there is between a short person and a tall person. However, there are very few examples of discontinuous variation in humans.

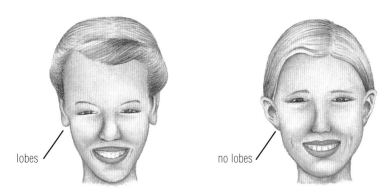

lobes   no lobes

Figure 4.24   Ears with and without ear lobes.

For discussion ·

Look at this photograph of a family. What features do the members of the family have in common? Which features are found in more than one generation?

Figure 4.25 Members of a family.

The causes of variation

Some members of the family in Figure 4.25 have similar features. They are found in different generations, which suggests that the features could be inherited. Some variations may also be due to the environment.

Variation and the environment

The environment can affect the features of a living organism. For example, if some seedlings of a plant are grown in the dark and some in the light they will have different features. Those grown in the dark will be tall, spindly and have yellow leaves, while those grown in the light will have shorter, firmer stems with larger leaves that are green.

Lack of minerals in the soil can affect the colour and structure of the leaves (see pages 156, 157). For example, the presence of lime in the soil affects the colour of hydrangea flowers. If the soil contains lime, the flowers are pink. If the soil is lime-free, the flowers are blue (see *Checkpoint Chemistry*).

The colour of flamingos is also affected by the environment. The flamingo feeds on shrimps that possess a pink pigment. The pigment passes into the feathers and makes the flamingo pink.

10 How else could the environment affect the development of an organism? Give another example for a plant and an animal.

Figure 4.26 Pink flamingos. When they do not eat enough shrimps their feathers become white.

Usually the food an animal eats affects the variation in the species. If the environment does not provide enough food, adult animals become thin and have a smaller body mass. Young animals grow slowly so they look smaller than other members of the species who have enough food and are the same age.

Usually animals eat only enough to keep them healthy and do not become too fat. However, animals which hibernate, like bats, or sleep for long periods of time through the winter, like bears, eat large amounts of food in the autumn and increase their body mass. The fat that they store provides them with enough energy to keep them alive while they are sleeping and not able to feed. When they emerge in the spring their body mass is greatly reduced.

Humans who eat too much food increase their body mass and this may threaten their health. The variation in body mass in a population in some countries is due to some people eating far too much.

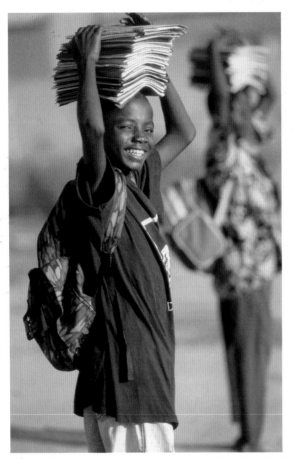 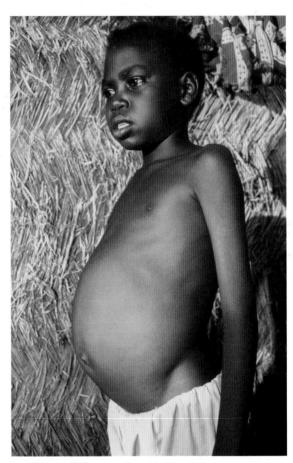

Figure 4.27 The child on the left has a healthy diet. The child on the right is suffering from kwashiorkor. He has been eating a starchy diet without protein, which has made his stomach swell.

◆ SUMMARY ◆

◆ Living things are classified by putting them into groups (*see page 44*).

◆ There are five kingdoms of living things. They are animals, plants, Monera, Protoctista and fungi (*see page 44*).

◆ There are four major classes of arthropods. They are the myriapods, the crustaceans, the arachnids and the insects (*see page 47*).

◆ There are five classes of vertebrates. They are fish, amphibians, reptiles, birds and mammals (*see page 49*).

◆ Viruses do not have a cell structure (*see page 51*).

◆ A species is a group of very similar organisms that can breed together and produce offspring which can also breed (*see page 51*).

◆ Keys are used to identify living things (*see page 52*).

◆ Some small animals may be kept in the laboratory and their behaviour can be studied by harmless experiments (*see page 57*).

◆ There is variation between species (*see page 58*).

◆ There are two kinds of variation within a species. They are continuous and discontinuous variation (*see page 59*).

◆ The environment can affect the variation in a species (*see page 60*).

End of chapter questions

1 What kind of living organisms are the following:
  a) does not have a backbone but has five arms,
  b) has a backbone and wings,
  c) does not have a backbone but has wings,
  d) has scales and lays eggs in water,
  e) has scales and lays eggs on land,
  f) has a backbone and hair?

2 Imagine that you have landed on a distant planet. When you climb out of your space craft you find some small eight-legged, six-eyed animals leaping about. You call them hoppys, and gather the information in Table 4.3 about twenty of them.
  a) Arrange the hoppys into five size groups based on their mass.
  b) Display the numbers in the groups in a bar chart.
  c) Arrange the hoppys into groups based on colour.
  d) Display the numbers in the groups in a bar chart.
  e) Which feature shows continuous variation?
  f) Which feature shows discontinuous variation?
  g) Is there any relationship between the mass of the hoppys and their colours? Describe what you find.
  h) Speculate on a reason for your findings.

Hoppy	Mass/g	Colour
1	200	green
2	349	green
3	210	green
4	615	blue
5	430	yellow
6	570	red
7	402	yellow
8	429	yellow
9	317	green
10	520	red
11	460	yellow
12	403	yellow
13	330	green
14	489	yellow
15	502	red
16	630	blue
17	410	yellow
18	380	green
19	550	red
20	445	yellow

Table 4.3

5 Habitats

If you look out across the countryside you may see fields, woods, ponds and maybe a river. Most of the living things you see will be plants ranging in size from green slime on rocks to the tallest tree in a wood. You may see some birds flying across the countryside and a few insects moving through the air around you. There may be a slug slowly moving across your path or a squirrel scampering away through the branches of a nearby tree. The scene may look too complicated to investigate scientifically, but the study of ecology was established at the beginning of the 20th Century to do just this.

1 What habitats can you see in Figure 5.1?

Figure 5.1 A scene from a tropical region of the Earth.

Ecology means the study of living things and where they live. The home area of a living thing is called its habitat. Two examples of habitats are a wood and a pond. The scene in Figure 5.1 can be divided into a number of different habitats for further investigation.

Daily adaptations in plants

The examples given are mainly found in northern Europe.

Flowers

Some plants such as the crocus and the tulip open their flowers during the day and close them at night. The flowers are open in the day so that insects may visit them for nectar, and in return transport pollen from one flower to another to bring about pollination. The flowers close at night to protect the delicate structures inside the petals from low temperatures and from dew. The dew could wash the pollen off the stamens (see page 143) so that it cannot be picked up and transported by the insects. The night scented stock is an unusual plant in that its flowers open in the evening and close during the day. This adaptation allows moths to visit the flowers and pollinate them.

Leaves

A few plants make movements of their leaves over a 24-hour period. Leaves not only make food but they also provide a large surface for the evaporation of water, which in turn helps to draw water through the plant from the roots. In clover, for example, each leaf is divided into three leaflets. During the day the leaflets spread out and become horizontal. In this position they are best placed for receiving sunlight to make food, and to lose water to the air, which causes the plant to draw up water from the roots. The water is needed to make food, and it also helps to keep the leaves cool in the sunlight. In the evening the leaflets fold close together. This helps them to lose less water when the plant is not making food.

The wood sorrel is another plant which moves its leaves over a 24-hour period. At night it lets its leaves droop to conserve water. Plants can make those movements by moving water about inside their bodies. When water is concentrated in one place it makes the cells swell up. When part of it is removed from a place the cells sag. This swelling and sagging of the cells allows the plants to move slowly.

2 Do the petals of a crocus and the leaves of a clover plant move for the same reason? Explain your answer.

For discussion
Consider local plants which show these adaptations.

Daily adaptation in animals

Animals are adapted to being active at certain times of the day and resting at other times. At night most birds roost (sleep) but as soon as it is light they may start flying about in search of food. They have large eyes and consequently have excellent vision, which is essential for them to fly, land and search for food.

The tawny owl has several adaptations that allow it to catch mice at night. It has large eyes that are sensitive to the low intensity of light in the countryside at night. These allow it to see to fly safely. The edges of some of the owl's wing feathers are shaped to move noiselessly through the air when the bird beats its wings. This prevents the mouse's keen sense of hearing from detecting the owl approaching in flight. The owl has sharp talons on its toes that act as daggers, to kill its prey quickly and to help carry the prey away to be eaten at a safe perch.

At night most birds are replaced in the air by bats. These animals roost in the day and come out at dusk to hunt for flying insects. Bats do not use their eyes but have developed an echo-location system. They send out very high-pitched squeaks that we cannot hear. These sounds reflect off all the surfaces around the bat and travel back to the bat's ears. The bat uses the information from these sounds to work out the distance, size and shape of objects around it. This allows the bat to fly safely and detect insects in the air, which it can swoop down and eat.

3 What adaptations does the tawny owl have that allow it to detect its prey, approach its prey and attack its prey?

4 Why should the owl kill its prey quickly?

5 What adaptations do you think a mouse may have to help it survive a predator's attack?

Figure 5.2   A tawny owl, swooping down on a wood mouse.

Many insects such as butterflies, bees and wasps are active and fly during the day. At night moths take to the air to search for food.

The squirrel is a mammal that is active during the day. Deer may also be active but they hide away in vegetation. Field mice and voles may be active during the day but hide in the grass and other low vegetation. These animals are also active for periods at night, when they are at risk of falling prey to night predators such as the fox and the owl.

While darkness is the major feature of a habitat at night there is also a second feature – humidity. At night all surfaces in the habitat cool down and the air cools down too. This causes water vapour in the air to condense and form dew. The increase in humidity is ideal for animals such as slugs and woodlice, which have difficulty retaining water in their bodies in dry conditions. They hide away in damp places during the day but as more places in the habitat become damp at night they become more active and roam freely searching for food. In the morning as the humidity decreases they hide away again somewhere damp.

Seasonal adaptations in plants

The abiotic non-living factors in a habitat change with the seasons. The grass plant is adapted to survive winter conditions but its short roots make it dependent upon the upper regions of the soil staying damp. In drought conditions the soil dries out and the grass dies. Daffodils are adapted to winter conditions as the leaves above the ground die and the plant forms a bulb in the soil. Bark is an adaptation of trees that provides a protective insulating layer around the woody shoot in winter.

Many trees have broad, flat leaves. They lose a great deal of water through them. In dry seasons or in regions where the ground freezes in winter and prevents water being taken up by the roots, the trees lose their leaves and grow new ones when conditions improve. These trees are called deciduous trees.

6 Imagine that you are camping in a wood.
   a) What animals may you expect to see during the day?
   b) What animals are active in the evening?

7 In what ways are plants adapted to survive winter conditions?

Figure 5.3 Deciduous trees.

Some trees, such as the holly and most conifers, have leaves that lose little water in winter. This allows the trees to stay in leaf all through the year. Trees which behave in this way are called evergreen trees.

Plants that float on the open water of a pond in spring and summer do not remain there in the winter.

Figure 5.4 Evergreen trees.

Duckweed produces individuals that sink to the pond floor; the water plant called frogbit produces heavy seeds. The plants around the water's edge die back and survive in the mud as thick stems called rhizomes.

Seasonal adaptations in animals

The roe deer (see Figure 5.5) lives in woodlands in Europe and Asia. In the spring and summer when the weather is warm it has a coat of short hair to keep it cool. In the autumn and winter it grows longer hair that traps an insulating layer of air next to its skin. This reduces the loss of heat from its body.

The stoat, which lives in northern Europe, northern Asia and Canada, grows a white coat in the winter which loses less heat than its darker summer coat. The stoat preys on rabbits and its white coat may also give it some camouflage when the countryside is covered in snow.

The ptarmigan is about the size of a hen. It lives in the north of Scotland, northern Europe and Canada. In summer it has a brown plumage that helps it hide away from predators while it nests and rears its young. In winter it has a white plumage that reduces the heat lost from its body and gives it camouflage. Feathers grow over its toes and make its feet into snowshoes which allow it to walk across the snow without sinking.

The lung fish of Africa and south America live in rivers, but when the rivers dry up in the dry season they can still survive. They make a burrow in the river bed

8 How do the adaptations of
   a) the roe deer,
   b) the stoat and
   c) the ptarmigan help them survive in the winter?

9 How might their winter adaptations affect their lives if they kept them through the spring and summer?

Figure 5.5 A roe deer in summer (left) and a ptarmigan in winter (right).

Figure 5.6 A lung fish out of water. It has a pair of lungs which it uses to extract oxygen from the air.

and rest there, breathing air until the rainy season returns. This kind of rest through a hot dry season is called aestivation.

In woodlands in Europe insects avoid harsh winter conditions by spending their lives in the inactive stages of their life cycles – the egg and the pupa.

This means that bats have nothing to eat in winter, so they store up fat in the autumn to give them energy to sleep though the winter in a state of hibernation.

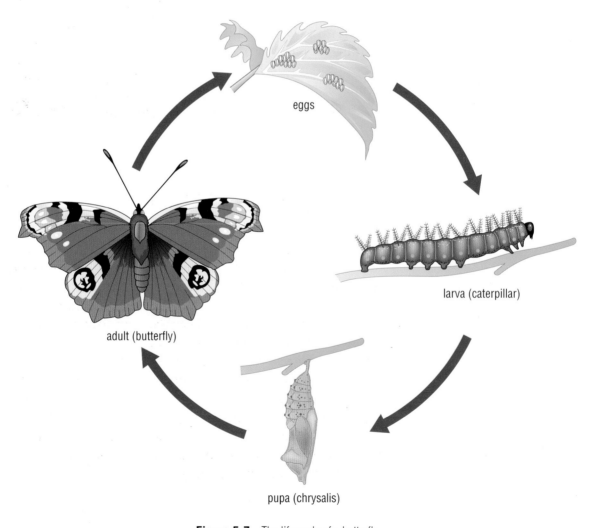

Figure 5.7 The life cycle of a butterfly.

Insect-eating birds such as the swallow leave the countries of northern Europe in the autumn and fly to Africa. They spend the winter feeding on insects in Africa, and return to Europe in the spring. When an animal moves its location as the seasons change it is said to migrate.

Figure 5.8 Swallows on migration.

For discussion

Which birds take part in migrations where you live? When do the migrations take place?

Investigating a habitat

A habitat, such as wood or a pond, is a home for a range of living things. When ecologists study a habitat they need to collect data about it. This not only provides information about the organisms that live there, but the data can also be stored and used to monitor the habitat in the following way. At a later date another survey can be made and the data obtained then can be compared with the previous data. This shows how the populations of species have fared in the time between the surveys. Some may have increased, others decreased and some stayed the same. By comparing data in this way the effects of events close by, such as a change in land use or the release of pollutants, can be carefully studied for signs of environmental damage.

Recording the plant life in a habitat

When a habitat is chosen for study a map is made in which the habitat boundaries and major features, such as roads or cliffs, are recorded. The main kinds of plants growing in the habitat are identified and the way they are distributed in the habitat is recorded on the map.

A more detailed study of the way the plants are distributed is made by using a quadrat and by making a transect.

Using a quadrat

A quadrat is a square frame. It is placed over an area of ground and the plants inside the frame are recorded. When using a quadrat the area of ground should not be chosen carefully. A carefully selected area might not give a fair record of the plant life in the habitat, but may support an idea that the ecologists have worked out beforehand. To make the test fair the quadrat is thrown over the shoulder so that it will land at random. The plants inside it are then recorded. This method is repeated a number of times and the results of the random samples are used to build up a record of how the plants are distributed. An estimate of how many of each kind there are in the area can then be made.

Figure 5.9 Ecologists mapping a habitat.

Figure 5.10 Ecologists using a quadrat.

10 How could you use a quadrat to see how the plants change in a particular area over a year?

Making a transect

If there is a feature such as a bank, a footpath or a hedge in the habitat, the way it affects plant life is investigated by using a line transect. The position of the transect is chosen carefully so that it cuts across the feature being examined.

The transect is made by stretching a length of rope along the line to be examined and recording the plants growing at certain intervals (called stations) along the rope. When plants are being recorded along a transect, abiotic factors such as temperature or dampness of the soil may also be recorded to see if there is a pattern between the way the plants are distributed and the varying abiotic factors.

Figure 5.11 Ecologists making a transect.

Collecting small animals

Different species of small animals live in different parts of a habitat. In a land habitat they can be found in the soil, on the soil surface and leaf litter, among the leaf blades and flower stalks of herbaceous plants, and on the branches, twigs and leaves of woody plants. They can be collected from each of these regions using special techniques.

Collecting from soil and leaf litter

A Tullgren funnel is used to collect small animals from a sample of soil or leaf litter. The sample is placed on a gauze above the funnel and a beaker of water is placed below the funnel. The lamp is lowered over the sample and switched on. The heat from the lamp dries the soil or leaf litter and the animals move downwards to the more moist regions below. Finally, the animals move out of the sample and into the funnel. The sides of the funnel are smooth so the animals cannot grip onto them and they fall into the water.

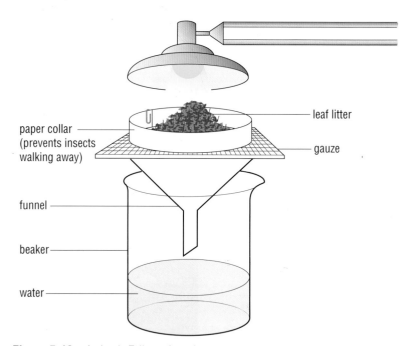

paper collar (prevents insects walking away)

leaf litter

gauze

funnel

beaker

water

Figure 5.12 A simple Tullgren funnel.

Pitfall trap

The pitfall trap is used to collect small animals that move over the surface of the ground. A hole is dug in the soil to hold two containers, such as yoghurt pots, arranged one inside the other. The containers are placed in the hole, and the gap around them up to the rim of the outer container is filled in with soil. A few small leaves are placed in the bottom of the container and four pebbles are placed in a square around the top of the trap. A piece of wood is put over the trap, resting on

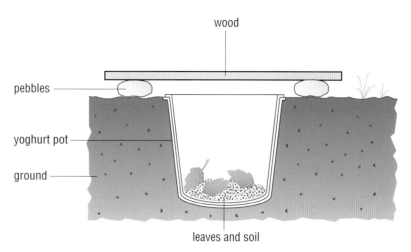

Figure 5.13 A pitfall trap.

11 What is the advantage of using an outer and an inner container instead of just one container for the pitfall trap?

12 Why are large leaves not used inside the trap?

the pebbles. The wood makes a roof to keep the rain out and hides the container from predators. When a small animal falls in it cannot climb the smooth walls of the inner container and remains in the trap, hiding under the leaves until the trap is emptied.

Sweep net

The sweep net is used to collect small animals from the leaves and flower stems of herbaceous plants, especially grasses. The lower edge of the net should be held slightly forward of the upper edge to scoop up the animals as the net is swept through the plants. After one or two sweeps the mouth of the net should be closed by hand and the contents emptied into a large plastic jar where the animals can be identified.

Figure 5.14 Using a sweep net.

Sheet and beater

Small animals in a bush or tree can be collected by setting a sheet below the branches and then shaking or beating the branches with a stick. The vibrations dislodge the animals, which then fall onto the sheet. The smallest animals can be collected in a pooter (Figure 5.15).

Pooter

13 What is the purpose of the cloth on tube B of the pooter?

Tube A of the pooter is placed close to the animal and air is sucked out of tube B. This creates low air pressure in the pooter so that air rushes in through tube A, carrying the small animal with it.

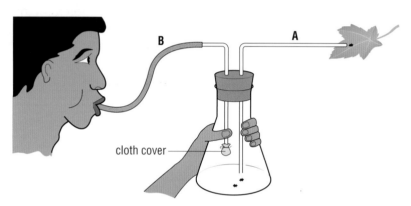

Figure 5.15 Using a pooter.

Collecting pond animals

Pond animals may be collected from the bottom of the pond, the water plants around the edges or the open water just below the surface.

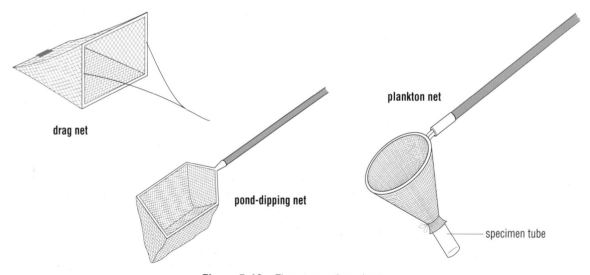

Figure 5.16 Three types of pond net.

A drag net is used to collect animals from the bottom of the pond. The net is dragged across the bottom of the pond. As it moves along it scoops up animals living on the surface of the mud. The pond-dipping net is used to sweep through vegetation around the edge of the pond to collect animals living on the leaves and stems. A plankton net is pulled through the open water to collect small animals swimming there.

Adaptations for feeding

There are two main ways in which animals are adapted for feeding. There are animals which are adapted for feeding on plant foods (these animals are called herbivores), and those that are adapted for feeding on other animals (carnivores).

Herbivores

When people think of herbivores they tend to think of herbivorous mammals such as the cow or the deer. Herbivores exist in other animal groups too. For example caterpillars, which are insects, and slugs and snails, which are molluscs, are all herbivores. Plant material is tough so herbivorous animals have adaptations that allow them to break it up for digestion. Herbivorous mammals such as cattle, sheep and antelope have large, strong back teeth that they use for grinding up the food. Caterpillars have strong jaws for nibbling along the edge of a leaf, while slugs and snails have a tongue covered in tiny teeth which they use like sandpaper to rasp away at the surface of their food.

Herbivorous animals are the prey of carnivorous animals, so they have developed features which help them reduce their chances of being caught and eaten. Many herbivores, from caterpillars to giraffes, have body colours which help them blend into their surroundings – they have camouflage.

Some herbivores, such as deer (see Figure 5.5 page 69), may also hide away during the day in vegetation and come out into the open at night when it is difficult for carnivores to see them.

Herbivorous mammals such as the rabbit (see Figure 4.23 page 58) have eyes on the sides of their head. This gives them a very wide field of vision, enabling them to see a carnivore approaching. Rabbits, like many herbivorous animals, have large ears which can be turned to face almost every direction so that the sound of an approaching predator can be detected.

14 a) Design a bark-feeding mammal that burrows its way from tree to tree.
   b) What adaptations would you give it to protect it from predators?

Figure 5.17 Giraffes are the tallest living animals. Their colouring is very similar to their surroundings and this helps to camouflage them.

Carnivores

Just as people think of a cow as a herbivore they may think that all carnivores are like the lion or leopard. Carnivores, like herbivores, come in all shapes and sizes. Spiders, for example, are carnivores. They set web traps to catch their prey. The frog is also a carnivore, and can flick out its tongue very quickly to catch flies. Most carnivorous mammals have large conical canine teeth (see page 105) for stabbing their prey, and molars which are adapted for holding bones while the jaw muscles press on them to crack them open for their marrow. The shrew belongs to a group of mammals which feed mainly on insects, called the insectivores. Its teeth are pointed, making the jaws look like those of a miniature crocodile. This arrangement of teeth allows the shrew to catch hold of the tough body of an insect and chew it up.

Animals which catch prey are called predators. Predatory birds such as eagles, hawks and owls are known as birds of prey and are adapted for catching and feeding on other animals. They have long claws on their feet called talons, which they use to grab and stab their prey. They also have hooked beaks for ripping up their prey into smaller pieces that are easy to swallow. Carnivorous birds and mammals share an adaptation.

15 Design a bird that feeds on the mammal you invented for Question 14. Explain the reasons for the features you give it.

16 A starling pulls up a worm and eats it. Later a sparrow hawk attacks and kills the starling and carries it away for a meal.

Do these observations support the idea that carnivores are always predators? Explain your answer.

They both have eyes that face forwards. This means that the field of view of each eye partly overlaps the field of view of the other eye, and this allows the animal to judge distance.

Figure 5.18 Lions have forward-facing eyes.

17 How does the field of vision of a herbivore (see page 77) compare with that of a carnivore?

Without this overlap judging distance can be very difficult. You can test this yourself by putting a pen and its top on the table. Close one eye, look at the two objects then pick them up and try quickly to put the top on the pen. The chances are that the first time you try this you will miss. Carnivorous animals need to be able to judge distance extremely accurately to pounce on their prey. If they miss, they go hungry.

As herbivorous mammals are constantly looking, listening and even sniffing the air for signs of an approaching predator, predators themselves have to take care when they are hunting. Some predators such as lions even set up an ambush to catch their prey.

Adapting to certain habitats

Deserts

In deserts there may be a short rainy season followed by a long dry season. Some flowering plants have very short life cycles so that they can germinate as soon as it rains. They can then grow, flower and set seed before the soil loses all of its moisture. Cacti survive dry conditions by storing water inside their bodies. They have a thick waxy covering to prevent the water from

Special relationships

A predator is a carnivore and the animal that it feeds on is its prey. A predator may have a wide range of prey. A weasel, for example, feeds on frogs, mice, voles, rats, small birds and moles. In the prey–predator relationship the predator survives by killing the prey. Young, old or sickly prey are the easiest animals to catch. The prey may sometimes try to avoid being caught by having camouflage or being able to move fast.

A parasite lives on or in another organism and feeds on it. The organism that contains the parasite is called the host. A head louse is an ectoparasite. It lives on the outside of the body and feeds on blood by piercing the skin on the scalp. The tapeworm is an endoparasite. It lives in the small intestine and feeds on the digested food. In the parasite–host relationship both organisms stay alive but the host is harmed (sometimes fatally) by the presence of the parasite. Some fungi are parasites on green plants and frequently kill them. Mistletoe is a green plant that is a semi-parasite. It has green leaves and can photosynthesise but it takes its minerals from the apple or poplar tree on which it is growing.

There are some organisms that are able to live apart but benefit when they live together. This relationship is called commensalism. Feeding may be only a part of this relationship. For example, the hermit crab often has sea anemones on its shell. They provide it with some camouflage and the messy feeding habits of the crab make a cloud of food particles in the water that the sea anemones can feed on.

Mutualism is a relationship where both organisms need each other to survive. The termite feeds on wood, which is made of cellulose. Protoctista that make an enzyme to digest cellulose live in the termite's gut. They allow the termite to digest the wood and in return the termite provides them with a home. The lichen is another example of mutualism. It consists of a fungus and an alga growing together. The fungus provides the support in which the alga can grow. The alga makes food by photosynthesis using the water that the fungus has stored. The fungus also takes in minerals to be converted into materials for growth. Together the two organisms form a structure that can live on the surfaces of rocks in harsh conditions where other organisms cannot survive.

1 Write down six examples of predators and their prey. For each pair say how each animal is adapted to catch prey or avoid being eaten.
2 Why is it a disadvantage if the parasite kills the host?
3 Why is mistletoe called a semi-parasite?
4 What is the difference between commensalism and mutualism?
5 How might a predator help the population of its prey?

Figure A   Head louse.

Figure B   Hermit crab with sea anemones on its shell.

For discussion
What clothes do people wear to help them survive in a desert? Explain how the clothes help the people to survive.

escaping from their surfaces, and spikes to prevent animals from biting into them for a drink. Some cacti have roots which spread out a long way just underneath the soil surface. They collect as much water as possible from the upper part of the soil when the rains arrive. Other cacti have long roots which grow deep into the soil to collect the water that has drained down there.

Figure 5.19 Cacti growing in a desert.

The camel has many adaptations for survival in the desert. After drinking a hundred litres of water it can walk for several days without taking another drink. Its feet have thick pads, which insulate it from the hot desert sand. The feet are also webbed so that their weight is spread out over a larger area. This reduces the pressure on the sand, and stops the camel from sinking into it. The camel has long legs, which hold the body above the hot air close to the ground. There are muscles in the camel's nose that enable it to shut its nostrils. This keeps sand out of the respiratory system during a sandstorm. The eyes have long lashes which keep flying sand from reaching the eyes in a sandstorm. If sand does get into an eye, camels have a third eyelid to get it out. It moves from side to side and wipes it away. It is so thin that a camel can see through it, and camels often keep this closed while walking through a sandstorm. Desert plants have tough leaves but the camel has strong teeth to grind them up. If the camel cannot find food it uses energy stored in the fat in its hump.

Figure 5.20

Mountains

The conditions on mountain tops are similar to conditions in the polar regions. There are long seasons when it is too cold for plants to grow and the ground is covered with snow, which makes it difficult for animals to move around and find food.

Plants on mountains may spend the cold season as seeds and sprout into life when warm conditions arrive. The plants complete their life cycles in a few weeks so that the seeds are ready for the next season of cold weather. Some plants survive the cold conditions by having hairy leaves. These hairs prevent the plants from losing water, and trap air to provide insulation. Mountain plants also grow close to the ground; if they grew tall they would be damaged by the frequent winds that blow around mountain tops.

18 A seed from a plant adapted for growing in lowland meadows is carried by the wind up a mountain and lands at its top. The seed then germinates and starts to grow in the warm season. What may happen to the plant when the cold season arrives? Explain your answer.

Figure 5.21 Moss campion is growing very low to the ground on this alpine surface. The flowers are produced on the side of the moss cushion that receives the most light.

Birds such as the golden eagle and raven visit the mountain tops in summer to look for food, but avoid them in winter. Large animals such as mountain goats and red deer also visit high mountainsides to feed on the plants, but move down the mountain before winter to avoid being trapped in the snow. The ptarmigan (see page 69) is a bird that remains on the mountains throughout the year. It changes its plumage to match its surroundings and avoid predators. The mountain hare also changes its colour from brown in summer to white in winter.

Figure 5.22   The mountain goat can find small spaces on rock faces in which to place its feet and keep its balance as it feeds.

Aquatic habitats

Aquatic habitats are watery habitats. There are freshwater habitats such as ponds and rivers, and salt water habitats such as seas and oceans and their sandy or rocky shores.

Freshwater habitats

Water plants

The roots of land plants have oxygen around them in the air spaces in the soil. In the waterlogged mud at the bottom of a pond there is very little oxygen for the root cells. The stems of water plants have cavities in them through which air can pass to the roots in order to overcome this problem.

19 In what ways are the features of a plant living in water different from a plant living on land?

Figure 5.23   A pond with a range of water plants.

Water plants use the gases they produce to hold their bodies up in the water and therefore do not need strong, supporting tissues, as land plants do. Minerals can be taken in from the water through the shoot surfaces of the water plant, leaving the root to act as an anchor. The leaves of submerged water plants are thin, allowing minerals in the water to pass into them easily. The leaves also have feathery structures that make a large surface area in contact with the water. This further helps the plant to take in all the essential minerals.

Floating water plants like duckweed have a root that acts as a stabiliser.

Water animals

Although it lives underwater the diving beetle breathes air. It comes to the surface and pushes the tip of its abdomen out of the water. The beetle raises its wing covers and takes in air through breathing holes, called spiracles, on its back. (In insects living on land the spiracles are on the side of the body.) When the beetle lowers its wing covers, more air is trapped in the hairs between them. It is able to breathe this air while it swims underwater. Diving beetles feed on a range of foods, including small fish, tadpoles and other insects.

Figure 5.24 A diving beetle feeding on an earthworm.

Salt water habitats

Algae

Algae are members of the Protoctista kingdom. Billions of algae live in the sunlit waters of seas and oceans. They contain drops of oil to help them float, and long spines to slow down the speed at which they sink. The more slowly they sink the greater the chance of a water current pushing them back up to near the surface. These algae make food by photosynthesis (see page 145), and so it is vital for them to remain in water which receives sunlight.

Seaweeds are large algae which live at the edges of seas and oceans and on rocky shores. They too must stay in sunlit water, but close to the shore are strong currents due to the tides. The seaweeds have root-like structures called holdfasts, which grip the rocks and stop the seaweeds from being swept away.

Figure 5.25 A fur seal diving around large seaweeds called kelp.

The seas and oceans are home to a great variety of animal species, and new species are discovered every year. Animals which live on the ocean floor such as the sea spider have long legs to help them walk over the mud. In the deep ocean water where sunlight does not reach, many animals have special organs to generate light. Light generated by living things is called bioluminescence. Very little heat is generated by the chemical reactions which produce light so the cells of the organism are not damaged. The light is used by the animals to recognise each other in the dark and to find food.

20 What might happen if living organisms that emit light energy also produced a large amount of heat energy?

Figure 5.26 A cuttlefish with light organs.

Animals on the sea shore are in danger of being swept away by water currents. Lugworms and molluscs such as cockles and razor shells burrow in sandy beaches to stay on the shore. The limpet has a fleshy foot which acts like a sucker to hold it in place on a rocky shore. Sea anemones also have a sucker-like base which helps them to grip the sides of a rock pool.

Figure 5.27   Sea anemones and limpets in a rock pool.

Looking for links between plants and animals

All the individuals of a species in a particular habitat make up a group called a population. All the populations of the different species in the habitat make up a group called a community. Ecologists look for links between the animals and plants in the community to understand how they live together.

Most animals spend a large part of their time searching for food. By observing animals in their habitat, the food of each species can be identified.

Living things can be grouped according to how they feed. Plants make their own food by photosynthesis and by taking in minerals. They are called the producers of food. Animals that feed on plants are called primary consumers. They are also known as herbivores. Animals that feed on primary consumers are called secondary consumers. They are also known as carnivores. The highest level consumer in a food chain is called the top carnivore. Some animals such as bears feed on both plants and animals. They are called omnivores. An omnivore feeds as a primary consumer when it feeds on plants, and as a secondary or higher level consumer when it feeds on animals.

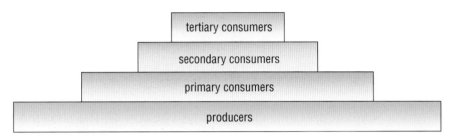

Figure 5.28 This diagram shows how the number of producers and consumers compare in a habitat. The bigger the block, the bigger the number of organisms.

21 In the food chain (right) identify
  a) the primary consumer,
  b) the secondary consumer and
  c) the tertiary consumer.
22 In the food chain (right) identify the herbivore and the carnivores.

23 Construct some food chains with humans in them.
24 In the food chains you have constructed are humans classed as herbivores, carnivores or omnivores?

Food chains

The information about how food passes from one species to another in a habitat is set out as a food chain. For example, it may be discovered that a plant is eaten by a beetle which in turn is eaten by a shrew and that the shrew is eaten by an owl. This information can be shown as follows:

plant → beetle → shrew → owl

Once a food chain has been worked out further studies can be done on the species in it.

Energy and the food chain

While animals need food substances from their meals to nourish their bodies, they also need energy to keep their bodies alive. The source of energy for almost all food chains is the Sun (for more details on the energy from the Sun see *Checkpoint Physics*). Some of the energy in sunlight is trapped in the leaves of plants and stored in food that the plant makes. When a herbivore eats the plant the energy is transferred to the body of the herbivore. Some of this energy is used up by the herbivore to keep it alive, but some is stored in its tissues. When a carnivore eats a herbivore it takes in the energy from the herbivore's body and uses it to keep itself alive. The food chain is an example of an energy transfer system.

A few food chains do not have the Sun as a source of energy. They are found around hot springs deep in the ocean. Some bacteria use hydrogen sulphide in the water as a source of energy, and crabs and worms feed on them.

◆ SUMMARY ◆

♦ The home of a living thing is called its habitat (*see page 64*).
♦ Some plants are adapted to changes that occur during the day (*see page 65*).
♦ Animals are adapted to changes that occur during the day (*see page 66*).
♦ Plants are adapted to changes that occur with the seasons (*see page 67*).
♦ Animals are adapted to changes that occur with the seasons (*see page 69*).
♦ Plant distribution can be examined using a quadrat and by making a transect (*see pages 72–73*).
♦ The Tullgren funnel, pitfall trap, sweep net, sheet and beater can be used to investigate small animals in a land habitat (*see pages 74–76*).
♦ Some animals are adapted for feeding on plants (*see page 77*).
♦ Some animals are adapted for feeding on other animals (*see page 78*).
♦ Some plants and animals are adapted for survival in a desert (*see page 79*).
♦ Some plants and animals are adapted for survival on mountains (*see page 82*).
♦ Some plants and animals are adapted for survival in freshwater (*see page 83*).
♦ Many organisms are adapted for survival in a salt water habitat (*see page 84*).
♦ Food passes from one species to another along a food chain (*see page 87*).
♦ A food chain is an energy transfer system (*see page 87*).

End of chapter questions

1 How would you set about investigating a habitat such as a hedgerow?
2 What surfaces do river limpets prefer? The river limpet lives in fast-flowing streams and rivers. There are many different surfaces on the bottom of a stream or river. This experiment was devised to test the results of observations in streams and rivers. The experiment also tested limpets of different sizes to see if larger ones had different preferences from smaller ones.

A 9 cm crystallising dish was divided into four sections called sectors. Each sector had one type of material, either sand, grit, stone or glass. The sectors were covered with water. Twelve limpets were used in each trial and there were two trials for each size class. New limpets were used for each trial. During each trial the number of limpets in each section was recorded after 30 minutes and 60 minutes. The results are displayed in Table 5.1.

(continued)

Table 5.1

Size class/ mm	30 minutes						60 minutes					
	Sand	Grit	Stone	Glass	Total Rough	Smooth	Sand	Grit	Stone	Glass	Total Rough	Smooth
3–4	5	1	9	9	6	18	3	0	15	6	3	21
4–5	1	1	17	5	2	22	0	0	19	5	0	24
5–6	1	1	17	5	2	22	0	0	20	4	0	24
6–7	2	3	11	8	5	19	0	0	21	3	0	24
Total	9	6	54	27	15	81	3	0	75	18	3	93

a) How many
   i) size classes were there?
   ii) trials were made in total?
   iii) limpets took part in the experiment?
b) After 30 minutes what can you conclude about the surface the limpets preferred?
c) What has happened in the crystallising dish during the period from 30 to 60 minutes?
d) What can you conclude about the limpets' surface preferences?
e) Do different sized limpets have different surface preferences?
f) A limpet has a 'foot' like a snail or slug. Why do you think it prefers the surfaces shown in the results?
g) If the experiment was extended to 2 hours what results would you predict?

3 The tufted hair grass forms a clump called a tussock. This provides a habitat for different kinds of invertebrates. The numbers of individuals of the different kinds of invertebrates were investigated over an 8-month period.

   Fifteen tussocks were dug up at random on a common each month and were taken apart carefully. The animals in each tussock were collected, arranged into groups and counted. The graphs in Figure 5.30 were produced from the data collected.

a) How did the numbers of butterflies and moths (larvae and pupae) change during the 8 months?
b) Describe the population of animals in the tussocks in April.
c) How did the population change by May?
d) Why were the tussocks picked at random?

The animals found in the tussocks of tufted hair grass were compared with those in the tussocks of cocksfoot grass in May. The results were displayed in a bar chart (Figure 5.29).

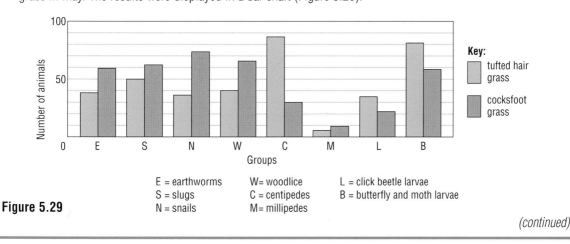

Figure 5.29

E = earthworms
S = slugs
N = snails
W = woodlice
C = centipedes
M = millipedes
L = click beetle larvae
B = butterfly and moth larvae

(continued)

e) What are the two most numerous groups of animals in
  i)   the tufted hair grass tussocks   ii)   the cocksfoot tussocks?
f) Which group of animals is found almost in the same numbers in both tussocks?
g) Which group of animals is twice as numerous in one type of tussock compared with the other?

The animals found in the tussocks of the cocksfoot grass in June were compared with those found in a rush tussock. The two pie charts in Figure 5.31 show how the populations compare.
h) What are the major ways in which the animal populations in the two tussocks differ?

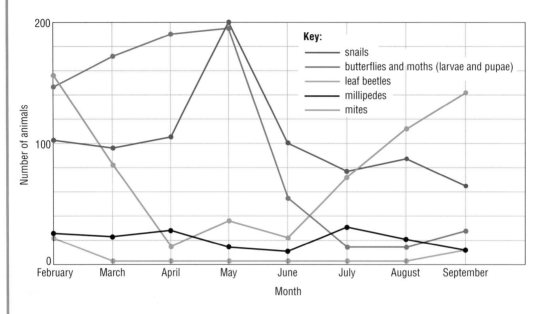

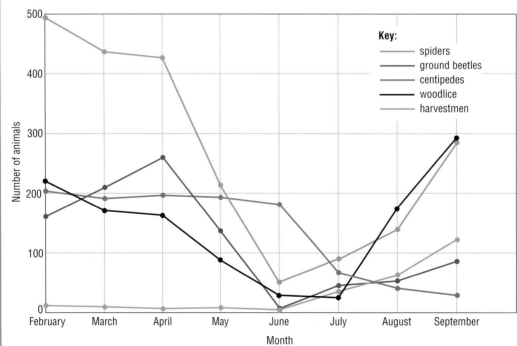

Figure 5.30

(continued)

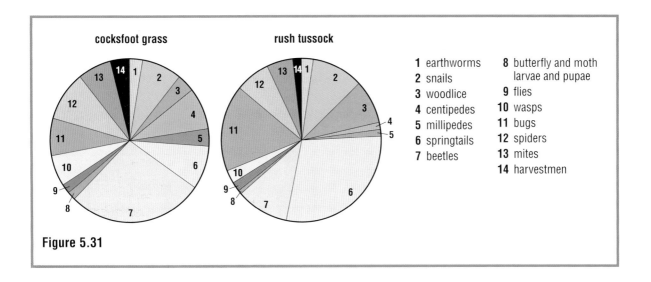

cocksfoot grass   **rush tussock**

1 earthworms
2 snails
3 woodlice
4 centipedes
5 millipedes
6 springtails
7 beetles

8 butterfly and moth larvae and pupae
9 flies
10 wasps
11 bugs
12 spiders
13 mites
14 harvestmen

Figure 5.31

6 | A healthy diet

Figure 6.1 Food for sale at a school canteen.

1 Write a description of your daily eating pattern.
2 Compare your pattern with the two on this page. Which one does your pattern resemble?
3 From what you already know, try to explain which diet is healthier.

For discussion

How healthy is your eating pattern? What changes would make it healthier? Do other people agree?

Some people do not eat breakfast. They may have some sweets on the way to school. At break they eat a chocolate bar or have a fizzy drink. At lunchtime they may have fried food such as potato chips with their meal. In the afternoon they have some more sweets, and for their evening meal they avoid green vegetables. Through the evening they have snacks of sweets, crisps and fizzy drinks.

Other people eat a breakfast of cereals and milk, toast and fruit juice. They eat an apple at break and have a range of lunchtime meals through the week which include different vegetables, pasta and rice. In the afternoon they may have an orange and eat an evening meal with green vegetables. They may have a milky drink at bedtime.

Nutrients

A chemical that is needed by the body to keep it in good health is called a nutrient. The human body needs a large number of different nutrients to keep it healthy. They can be divided up into the following nutrient groups:

- carbohydrates
- fats
- proteins
- vitamins
- minerals

In addition to these nutrients the body also needs water. It accounts for 70% of the body's weight and provides support for the cells, it carries dissolved materials around the body and it helps in controlling body temperature. Fibre is also needed by the body.

Carbohydrates

Carbohydrates are made from the elements carbon, hydrogen and oxygen. The atoms of these elements are linked together to form molecules of sugar. There are different types of sugar molecule but the most commonly occurring is glucose. Glucose molecules link together in long chains to make larger molecules such as starch. Glucose and starch are two of the most widely known carbohydrates but there are others, such as cellulose.

in starch, each of these links is a glucose molecule

Figure 6.2 Carbohydrate molecule.

Fats

Fats are made of large numbers of carbon and hydrogen atoms linked together into long chains together with a few oxygen atoms. There are two kinds of fats – the solid fats produced by animals, such as lard, and the liquid fat or oil produced by plants, such as sunflower oil.

Proteins

Proteins are made from atoms of carbon, hydrogen, oxygen and nitrogen. Some proteins also contain sulphur and phosphorus. The atoms of these elements join together to make molecules of amino acids. Amino acids link together into long chains to form protein molecules.

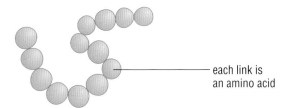

each link is an amino acid

Figure 6.3 Protein molecule.

4 What elements are found in carbohydrates, fats and proteins?

5 Which two words are used to describe the structure of carbohydrate, fat and protein molecules?

6 A science teacher held up a necklace of beads to her class and said it was a model of a protein molecule. What did each bead represent?

Vitamins

Unlike carbohydrates, fats and proteins, which are needed by the body in large amounts, vitamins are needed in only small amounts. When the vitamins were first discovered they were named after letters of the alphabet. Later, when the chemical structure of their molecules had been worked out, they were given chemical names.

Minerals

The body needs 20 different minerals to keep healthy. Some minerals, such as calcium, are needed in large amounts but others, such as zinc, are needed in only tiny amounts and are known as trace elements.

How the body uses nutrients

Carbohydrates

Carbohydrates contain a large amount of energy that can be released quickly inside the body. They are used as fuels to provide the energy for keeping the body alive.

Fibre

Cellulose is a carbohydrate which makes up the walls of plant cells. The cellulose in food is known as dietary fibre. It is found in foods such as wholemeal bread, fruit and vegetables. We cannot digest fibre, but it helps to move food along the intestines. As the fibre moves through the large intestine bacteria feed on it, and together the fibre and bacteria add bulk to the food. This helps the muscles of the large intestine push the food along. Fibre also takes up water like a sponge, and this makes the undigested foods which form the faeces soft and easy to release from the body. If a person's diet lacks fibre they may suffer from bowel problems such as constipation.

Nutrition		
Typical Composition	This pack (450g) provides	100g (3¹/₂oz) provide
Energy	2610kJ	580kJ
	621kcal	138kcal
Protein	13.2g	2.9g
Carbohydrate	82.3g	18.3g
of which sugars	18.0g	4.0g
Fat	26.6g	5.9g
of which saturates	13.5g	3.0g
mono-unsaturates	10.4g	2.3g
polyunsaturates	2.7g	0.6g
Fibre	7.2g	1.6g
Sodium	1.8g	0.4g
A serving (450g) contains the equivalent of approx. 4.5g of salt.		

Figure 6.4 The nutrients in a food product are displayed on the side of the packet.

Fats

Fats are needed for the formation of cell membranes. They also contain even larger amounts of energy than carbohydrates. The body cannot release the energy in fats as quickly as the energy in carbohydrates, so fats are used to store energy. In mammals the fat forms a layer under the skin. This acts as a heat insulator and helps to keep the mammal warm in cool conditions. Many mammals increase their body fat in the autumn so that they can draw on the stored energy if little food can be found in the winter. Some plants store oil in their seeds.

Proteins

Proteins are needed for building the structures in cells and in the formation of tissues and organs. They are needed for the growth of the body, to repair damaged parts such as cut skin, and to replace tissues that are constantly being worn away, such as the lining of the mouth.

Chemicals that take part in the reactions for digesting food and in speeding up reactions inside cells are called enzymes. These are also made from proteins.

Vitamins

Each vitamin has one or more uses in the body. Vitamin A is involved in allowing the eyes to see in dim light and in making a mucus lining to the respiratory, digestive and excretory systems which protects against infection from microorganisms.

There are several B vitamins of which vitamin B_1 (thiamin) is an example (see page 96).

A lack of vitamin C causes the deficiency disease called scurvy. As the disease develops bleeding occurs at the gums in the mouth, under the skin and into the joints. Death may occur owing to massive bleeding in the body.

Vitamin D helps the body take up calcium from food to make strong bones and teeth. Children who have a lack of vitamin D in the diet develop the deficiency disease called rickets, in which the bones do not develop to their full strength and may therefore bend. This is seen particularly in the leg bones. Look at the X-ray in Figure 6.5.

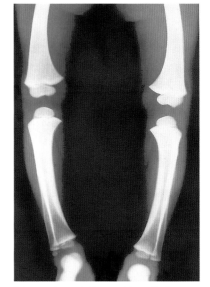

Figure 6.5 This child is suffering from rickets. It can be prevented by adding vitamin D to the diet.

Table 6.1 Vitamins and their uses.

Vitamin	Effect on body	Good sources
A	Increased resistance to disease Helps eyes to see in the dark	Milk, liver, cod-liver oil
B_1	Prevents digestive disorders Prevents the disease beriberi	Bread, milk, brown rice, soyabean, potato
C	Prevents the disease scurvy in which gums bleed and the circulatory system is damaged	Blackcurrant, orange, lemon, papaya, guava
D	Prevents the disease rickets in which bones become soft and leg bones of children may bend	Egg yolk, butter, cod-liver oil, pilchard, herring, sunlight

Finding the cause of beriberi

Christiaan Eijkman (1858–1930) was a Dutch doctor who worked at a medical school in the East Indies in the late 19th Century. He investigated the disease called beriberi. In this disease the nerves fail to work properly and the action of the muscles becomes weak. All movements, especially walking, become difficult, and as the disease progresses the heart may stop.

At this time other scientists had recently shown that microorganisms cause a number of diseases. It seemed reasonable to think that beriberi was also caused by a microorganism of some kind. Eijkman set up some investigations to find it. He was not having any success. Then one day a flock of chickens that were kept at the medical school began to show the symptoms of beriberi.

Figure A   A flock of hens with beriberi.

Eijkman tested them for signs of the microorganisms that he believed were causing the disease. Again he had no success in linking the disease to the microorganisms, but while he was studying the chickens they recovered from the disease. Eijkman began to search for a reason why they had developed the disease and also why they had recovered so quickly. He discovered that the chickens were usually fed on chicken feed (a specially prepared mixture of foods that kept them healthy). A cook who had been working at the medical school had stopped using the chicken feed and had fed the chickens on rice that had been prepared for the patients. This cook had left and a new cook had been employed who would not let the rice be fed to the chickens. The birds were once again fed on the chicken feed. When Eijkman fed the chickens on rice again they developed beriberi. When he fed them on chicken feed they recovered from the disease straight away.

The rice fed to the chickens and the patients was polished rice. This had had its outer skin removed and appeared white. Later work by scientists showed that the skin of the rice contained vitamin B_1 or thiamin. This vitamin is needed to keep the nerves healthy and prevent beriberi.

1 What are the symptoms of beriberi?
2 How serious is the disease?
3 Why did Eijkman begin by looking for microorganisms as a cause of beriberi?
4 In what way did chance play a part in the discovery of the cause of beriberi? Explain your answer.
5 Write down a plan of an investigation to check Eijkman's work on chickens and beriberi. How would you make sure it was fair and that the results were reliable?
6 How did Eijkman's work alter the way scientists thought diseases developed?
7 What is the danger in having a diet which mainly features polished rice? Explain your answer.

For discussion

Eijkman performed his experiments on animals. Question 5 asked you to plan an investigation to check his work. Your plan may have featured studying animals. A great deal of information that benefits humans has been gathered by studying animals in experiments. Are there any guidelines that you would want scientists to follow in experiments involving animals?

7 A meal contains carbohydrate, fat, protein, vitamin D, calcium and iron. What is the fate of each of these substances in the body?

8 Which carbohydrate cannot be digested by humans, and how does it help the digestive system?

9 In a patient suffering from rickets why do the leg bones bend more than the arm bones?

10 A seal is a mammal. How can it survive in the cold polar seas when a human would die in a few minutes?

Figure 6.6 Seals on the ice.

Minerals

Each mineral may have more than one use. For example, calcium is needed to make strong bones and teeth. It is also used to make muscles work and for blood to clot. A lack of calcium in the diet can lead to weak bones and high blood pressure. The mineral iron is used to make the red blood pigment called haemoglobin.

Water

About 70% of the human body is water. The body can survive for only a few days without a drink of water.

Every chemical reaction in the body takes place in water. The blood is made mainly from water. It is the liquid that transports all the other blood components around the body.

Water is used to cool down the body by the evaporation of sweat from the skin.

The amounts of nutrients in food

The amounts of nutrients in foods have been worked out by experiment and calculation. The amounts are usually expressed for a sample of food weighing 100 g. Table 6.2 shows the nutrients in a small range of common foods.

Table 6.2 The nutrients in some common foods.

Food (100 g)	Protein (g)	Fat (g)	Carbohydrate (g)	Calcium (mg)	Iron (mg)	Vitamin C (mg)	Vitamin D (µg)
Potato	2.1	0	18.0	8	0.7	8–30	0
Carrot	0.7	0	5.4	48	0.6	6	0
Bread	9.6	3.1	46.7	28	3.0	0	0
Spaghetti	9.9	1.0	84.0	23	1.2	0	0
Rice	6.2	1.0	86.8	4	0.4	0	0
Lentil	23.8	0	53.2	39	7.6	0	0
Pea	5.8	0	10.6	15	1.9	25	0
Jam	0.5	0	69.2	18	1.2	10	0
Peanut	28.1	49.0	8.6	61	2.0	0	0
Lamb	15.9	30.2	0	7	1.3	0	0
Milk	3.3	3.8	4.8	120	0.1	1	0.05
Cheese 1	25.4	35.4	0	810	0.6	0	0.35
Cheese 2	15.3	4.0	4.5	80	0.4	0	0.02
Butter	0.5	81.0	0	15	0.2	0	1.25
Chicken	20.8	6.7	0	11	1.5	0	0
Egg	12.3	10.9	0	54	2.1	0	1.50
Fish 1	17.4	0.7	0	16	0.3	0	0
Fish 2	16.8	18.5	0	33	0.8	0	22.20
Apple	0.3	0	12.0	4	0.3	5	0
Banana	1.1	0	19.2	7	0.4	10	0
Orange	0.8	0	8.5	41	0.3	50	0

Notes for Tables 6.2 and 6.3

Vegetables are raw; the bread is wholemeal bread; cheese 1 is cheddar cheese; cheese 2 is cottage cheese; fish 1 is a white fish, such as cod; fish 2 is an oily fish, such as herring.

Keeping a balance

In order to remain healthy the diet has to be balanced with the body's needs. A balanced diet is one in which all the nutrients are present in the correct amounts to keep the body healthy. You do not need to know the exact amounts of nutrients in each food to work out whether you have a healthy diet. A simple way is to look at a chart showing food divided into groups, with the main nutrients of each group displayed (see Table 6.4 page 100). You can then see if you eat at least one portion from each group each day and more portions of the food groups that lack fat. Remember that you also need to include fibre even though it is not digested. It is essential for the efficient working of the muscles in the alimentary canal. Fibre is found in cereals, vegetables and pulses, such as peas and beans.

11 In Table 6.2, which foods contain the most
  a) protein,
  b) fat,
  c) carbohydrate,
  d) calcium,
  e) iron,
  f) vitamin C and
  g) vitamin D?

12 Which foods would a vegetarian not eat?

13 Which foods would a vegetarian have to eat more of and why?

14 Which food provides all the nutrients?

15 Why might you expect this food to contain so many nutrients?

16 Table 6.3 shows the amount of energy provided by 100 g of each of the foods shown in Table 6.2. Arrange the nine highest energy foods in order, starting with the highest and ending with the lowest. Look at the nutrient content of these foods in Table 6.2.
  a) Do you think the energy is stored as fat or as carbohydrate in each of the nine highest energy foods?
  b) Arrange the foods into groups according to where you think the energy is stored.
  c) Do the food stores you have identified store the same amount of energy (see also page 94)? Explain your answer.

17 Why might people who are trying to lose weight eat cottage cheese instead of cheddar cheese?

18 Mackerel is an oily fish. Describe the nutrients you would expect it to contain.

Table 6.3 The energy value of some common foods.

Food (100 g)	Energy (kJ)
Potato	324
Carrot	98
Bread	1025
Spaghetti	1549
Rice	1531
Lentil	1256
Pea	273
Jam	1116
Peanut	2428
Lamb	1388
Milk	274
Cheese 1	1708
Cheese 2	480
Butter	3006
Chicken	602
Egg	612
Fish 1	321
Fish 2	970
Apple	197
Banana	326
Orange	150

19 Look again at the eating pattern you prepared for Question 1 on page 92. Analyse your diet into the food groups shown in Table 6.4. How well does your diet provide you with all the nutrients you need?

20 Table 6.5 shows how the energy requirements of an average male and female person change from the age of 2 to 25 years. Plot graphs of the information given in the table.

21 Describe what the graphs show.

22 Explain why there is a difference in energy needs between a 2-year-old child and an 8-year-old child.

23 Explain why there is a difference in energy needs between an 18-year-old male and an 18-year-old female.

24 Explain why there is a change in the energy needs as a person ages from 18 to 25.

25 What changes would you expect in the energy used by:
   a) a 25-year-old person who changed from a job delivering mail to working with a computer
   b) a 25-year-old person who gave up working with computers and took a job on a building site that involved carrying heavy loads
   c) a 25-year-old female during pregnancy?

26 What happens in the body if too much fat, carbohydrate or protein is eaten?

27 Why do people become thin if they do not eat enough high-energy food?

Table 6.4 The groups of foods and their nutrients.

Vegetables and fruit	Cereals	Pulses	Meat and eggs	Milk products
Carbohydrate	Carbohydrate	Carbohydrate	Protein	Protein
Vitamin A	Protein	Protein	Fat	Fat
Vitamin C	B vitamins	B vitamins	B vitamins	Vitamin A
Minerals	Minerals	Iron	Iron	B vitamins
Fibre	Fibre	Fibre		Vitamin C
				Calcium

Table 6.5 Average daily energy used by males and females.

| Age (years) | Daily energy used (kJ) | |
	Male	Female
2	5500	5500
5	7000	7000
8	8800	8800
11	10 000	9200
14	12 500	10 500
18	14 200	9600
25	12 100	8800

Malnutrition

If the diet provides too few nutrients or too many nutrients malnutrition occurs. Lack of a nutrient in a diet may produce a deficiency disease, such as scurvy or anaemia. Scurvy is a deficiency disease caused by a lack of vitamin C and anaemia is a deficiency disease caused by a lack of iron.

If more protein than is needed is eaten, it is broken down in the body. Part of it is converted to a carbohydrate called glycogen, which is stored in the liver, and part of it is converted to a chemical called urea, which is excreted in the urine.

Too much high-energy food such as carbohydrate and fat leads to the body becoming overweight. If the body is extremely overweight it is described as obese. If too little high-energy food is eaten the body becomes thin because it uses up energy stored as fat. Energy stored in protein in the muscles can also be used up.

The condition anorexia nervosa can lead to extreme weight loss and possibly death. It occurs mainly in teenage girls but is occurring increasingly in teenage boys and adult men and women. People suffering from anorexia nervosa eat very little and fear gaining weight. As soon as the condition is diagnosed, they need careful counselling to stand the best chance of making a full recovery.

A healthy diet

The body needs a range of nutrients to keep healthy (see pages 92–97) and everyone should eat a balanced diet to provide these nutrients. Regular eating of high-energy snacks, such as sweets, chocolate, crisps, ice-cream and chips, between meals unbalances the diet and can lead to the body becoming overweight, damage to the teeth (see pages 104–105) and ill-health. Overweight people have to make more effort than normal to move so they tend to take less exercise. In time this can affect the heart (see page 120).

High-energy snacks should be kept to a minimum so that the main meals of the day, which provide most of the essential nutrients, may be eaten. There are alternatives to high-energy snacks. These are fruits and raw vegetables, such as celery, tomatoes and carrots. In addition to being lower in energy they also provide more vitamins and minerals. You can think about the amounts of food you eat in the following way.

You can eat large amounts of potatoes, bread, rice and pasta. They provide you with carbohydrates, which supply the body with energy. You should eat a smaller amount of fruit and vegetables (but still five portions a day) to provide you with vitamins, minerals and fibre. You should eat a smaller amount still of foods such as meat and fish, to provide you with the protein you need for growth and repair of the body. In a vegetarian diet protein is mainly provided by pulses such as beans, lentils and peas. Finally you should eat even smaller amounts of food rich in fat such as chocolate, nuts, fatty meat and cheese. Fat provides materials for making cell membranes. It also creates an insulating layer beneath the skin that helps to retain body heat. This layer acts as an energy store for the body, but there can be dangers to health if it becomes too thick.

An easy way to think about all this information is to think of a pyramid of food, as Figure 6.7 shows.

28 Make a pyramid of food representing your diet. Describe how it compares with the pyramid in Figure 6.7. If it does not match the pyramid in the diagram, how can you change your diet to make it healthier?

Note: this pyramid of food is simply to make you think about eating healthily. It is not related to ecological pyramids found on page 87.

Figure 6.7 A pyramid of food.

The pyramid reminds you that you should eat large amounts of foods at the bottom of the pyramid but only small amounts of those at the top.

♦ SUMMARY ♦

♦ A chemical that is needed by the body to keep it healthy is called a nutrient (*see page 92*).

♦ The groups of nutrients are carbohydrates, fats, proteins, vitamins and minerals (*see page 92*).

♦ Each nutrient has a specific use in the body (*see page 94*).

♦ Fibre and water and are essential components of the diet (*see pages 94, 97*).

♦ Different foods have different amounts of nutrients (*see page 98*).

♦ A balanced diet needs to be eaten for good health (*see page 99*).

♦ Malnutrition occurs when a diet provides too few or too many nutrients (*see page 100*).

♦ You must eat different amounts of certain foods to have a healthy diet (*see page 101*).

End of chapter questions

1 What is a healthy diet?

2 We know that humans prefer certain foods but do animals? An investigation was done with a pair of zebra finches to find out. The zebra finches were tested with a seed mixture bought from a pet shop to see if they preferred to eat certain seeds in the mixture. A sample of the mixture was left in a dish in the birds' cage for 6 hours. At the end of that time the sample was removed and the seeds were separated into their different types. A sample of the original mixture, called the bulk, that was similar in size to the dish sample was also sorted into the different seed types.

Table 6.6

	Type A Millet	Type B Round brown seeds	Type C Elongate grey seeds	Type D Small round seeds	Type E Black seeds
Dish (total sample = 218)	25	39	27	124	3
Bulk (total sample = 288)	120	27	41	97	3

Table 6.6 shows the composition of the two samples. Table 6.7 shows the percentage of each type of seed in the two samples.

Table 6.7

	Type A	Type B	Type C	Type D	Type E
Dish (D)	12	14	13	59	1.5
Bulk (B)	42	9	14	34	1
Difference (D – B)	−30	+5	−1	+25	−0.5

a) Why was the dish sample left for 6 hours in the bird cage?

b) How was the test made fair?

c) Why could the figures for the seeds in the two samples in Table 6.6 not be compared directly?

d) How is the percentage of the seed type worked out?

e) Check the percentage of millet in both samples. How have the figures been processed?

f) If the dish sample had roughly the same composition as the bulk sample when it was first put in the birds' cage,

　i) which seeds have the birds eaten, and

　ii) which have they most strongly avoided?

g) How could you find out more about the birds' food preferences?

7

Digestion

Your food comes from the tissues of animals and plants. To enter the cells of your body the tissues have to be broken down. This releases the nutrients (carbohydrates, proteins, fats, minerals and vitamins). Some of them are in the form of long-chain molecules. They must be broken down into smaller molecules that dissolve in water and can pass through the wall of the gut. This process of making the food into a form that can be taken into the body is called digestion. It takes place in the digestive system, which is made up of the alimentary canal and organs such as the liver and pancreas.

The breakdown of food

There are two major processes in the breakdown of food. They are the physical and the chemical breakdown of food. Food is physically broken down from large objects into small objects in the mouth. Chemical breakdown begins in the mouth and continues along the alimentary canal.

The physical breakdown of food

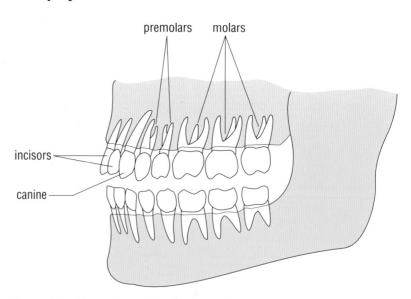

Figure 7.1 The four types of teeth in the mouth.

The teeth play a major part in the physical breakdown of food. There are four kinds of teeth. The chisel-shaped incisor teeth are at the front of the mouth. These are for biting into soft foods like fruits. Next to the incisors are the canines. These are pointed, and in dogs and cats they form the fang teeth that are used for tearing into tougher food like meat. Humans do not eat much tough food so they use their canines as extra incisors. The premolars and the molars are similar in appearance. They have raised parts called cusps with grooves between them. They form a crushing and grinding surface at the back of the mouth. The action of the teeth breaks up the food into small pieces.

The chemical breakdown of food

Proteins, fats and carbohydrates are made from large molecules which are made from smaller molecules that are linked together. The large molecules do not dissolve in water and cannot pass through the lining of the digestive system into the body. The smaller molecules from which they are made, however, *do* dissolve in water and *do* pass through the wall of the digestive system. Almost all reactions in living things involve chemicals called enzymes. They are made by the body from proteins and they speed up chemical reactions. Digestive enzymes speed up the breakdown of the large molecules into smaller ones.

1 Which smaller molecules join together to form
a) carbohydrates and
b) protein (see also page 93)?
2 What do enzymes in the digestive system do?

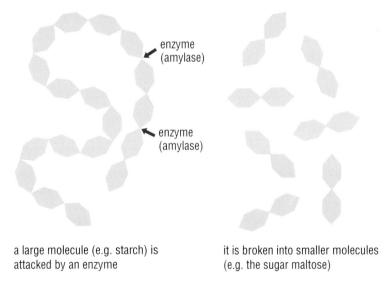

enzyme (amylase)

enzyme (amylase)

a large molecule (e.g. starch) is attacked by an enzyme

it is broken into smaller molecules (e.g. the sugar maltose)

Figure 7.2   The action of an enzyme on a large food molecule.

Early ideas about digestion

At one time there were two ideas about how food was digested. Some scientists believed that the stomach churned up the food to break it up physically and others believed that a chemical process took place.

Andreas Vesalius (1514–1564) was a Flemish doctor who investigated the structure of the human body by dissection. He had an artist make drawings of his work and these were published in a book for others to study.

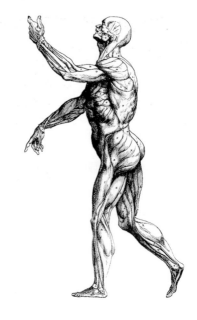

Figure A   A drawing of Vesalius's work.

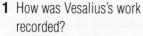

1 How was Vesalius's work recorded?
2 How life-like were the recordings of Vesalius's work?
3 How did the idea that the stomach acted as a churning machine develop?
4 If Borelli's idea had been correct what would Réaumur have found?
5 What did Réaumur's investigation show?
6 Do you think Réaumur's investigation threatened the hawk's life? Explain your answer.

René Descartes (1596–1650) studied mathematics and astronomy. He believed that all actions were due to mechanical movements. When he saw the drawings of Vesalius's dissections he believed that the human body behaved just as a machine.

Giovanni Borelli (1608–1679) studied the parts of the body and Descartes's ideas. He showed how muscles pulled on bones to make them move and how the bones acted as levers. This work supported Descartes's ideas, and Borelli extended it to consider the stomach as a churning machine for breaking up food.

Franciscus Sylvius (1614–1672), a German doctor, believed that chemical processes took place in the body and that digestion was a chemical process that began in the mouth with the action of saliva. Some other scientists believed in his ideas.

Figure B   A hawk eating a meal.

In 1752 René Réaumur (1683–1757), a French scientist, decided to test these two ideas by studying the digestion in a hawk. When a hawk feeds it swallows large pieces of its prey, digests the meat and regurgitates fur, feathers and bones that it cannot digest. Réaumur put some meat inside small metal cylinders and covered the ends with a metal gauze. He fed the cylinders to the hawk and waited for the hawk to regurgitate them. He found that some of the meat had dissolved but the cylinders and gauze showed no signs of being ground up as if by a machine. To follow up his experiment he fed a sponge to the hawk to collect some of the stomach juices. When the hawk regurgitated the sponge Réaumur squeezed out the stomach juices and poured them on to a sample of meat. Slowly the meat dissolved.

Along the alimentary canal

When your mouth waters

The 'water' that occurs in your mouth is called saliva. You can make up to $1\frac{1}{2}$ litres of saliva in 24 hours. Saliva is made by three pairs of salivary glands. The glands are made up of groups of cells that produce the saliva, and ducts (tubes) that deliver it to the mouth.

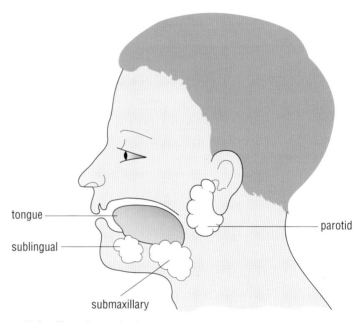

Figure 7.3 The salivary glands.

Saliva is 99% water but it also contains a slimy substance called mucin and an enzyme called amylase which begins the digestion of starch in the food. The mucin coats the food and makes it easier to swallow. Amylase begins the breakdown of starch molecules into sugar molecules.

When you swallow

When you have chewed your food it is made into a pellet called the bolus. This is pushed to the back of your mouth by your tongue. Swallowing causes the bolus to slide down your gullet, which is the tube connecting the mouth to the stomach. This tube is also called the oesophagus. It has two layers of muscles in its walls.

In the outer layer the muscle cells are arranged so that they point along the length of the gullet. These form the longitudinal muscle layer. In the inner layer the cells are arranged so that they point around the wall of the gullet. These form the circular muscle layer.

3 How does saliva help in digesting food?

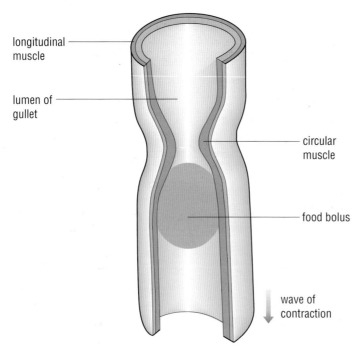

longitudinal muscle

lumen of gullet

circular muscle

food bolus

wave of contraction

Figure 7.4 The structure of the gullet and the process of peristalsis.

Muscle cells can contract (get shorter). They cannot lengthen on their own, so another set of muscle cells must work to lengthen them. In the gullet, when the circular muscles contract, they squeeze on the food and push it along the tube. The longitudinal muscles then contract to stretch the circular muscles once again. The circular muscles do not all contract at the same time. Those at the top of the gullet contract first then a region lower down follows and so on until the food is pushed into the stomach. This wave of muscular contraction is called peristalsis. Peristaltic waves also occur in other parts of the alimentary canal to push the food along.

Stomach

The stomach wall is lined with glands. These produce hydrochloric acid and a protein-digesting enzyme called pepsin. The hydrochloric acid kills many kinds of bacteria in the food and provides the acid conditions that pepsin needs to start breaking down protein in the food.

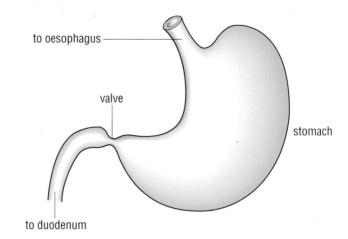

to oesophagus

valve

stomach

to duodenum

4 What is peristalsis?
5 What does hydrochloric acid do?

Figure 7.5 The stomach.

A hole in the stomach

In 1822 a group of fur trappers and hunters gathered at a trading post, Fort Mackinac, USA. One of the hunters accidentally fired his gun and shot a 19-year-old man called Alexis St Martin. It was fortunate that Doctor William Beaumont (1785–1853) was close by and could attend to the wounded man and save his life. St Martin had lost some flesh from over his stomach and part of the stomach wall. The wound did not completely heal. It formed a flap over the stomach which could be opened and the contents of the stomach examined.

St Martin agreed to help Beaumont to find out what happened inside the stomach during digestion. First Beaumont asked St Martin to eat nothing for a few hours then he looked inside the stomach and found that the stomach contained saliva, which St Martin had swallowed, and some mucus from the stomach wall.

In another experiment Beaumont put some bread crumbs into the stomach and saw digestive juice start to collect on the wall of the stomach.

Beaumont wanted to find out what happened to food in the stomach. So, he fastened pieces of cooked and raw meat, bread and cabbage onto silk strings and pushed them through the hole. An hour later he pulled the strings out and found that about half the cabbage and bread had broken up but the meat remained the same. Another hour later he found that the cooked meat had started to break down.

Next Beaumont wanted to find out what happened to the food after St Martin had eaten it. He gave St Martin a meal of fish, potatoes, bread and parsnips. After half an hour Beaumont examined the stomach contents and found that he could still identify pieces of fish and potato. After another half hour pieces of potato could still be seen but most of the fish had broken up. One and a half hours after the meal all the pieces of the food had broken up. Two hours after the meal the stomach was empty.

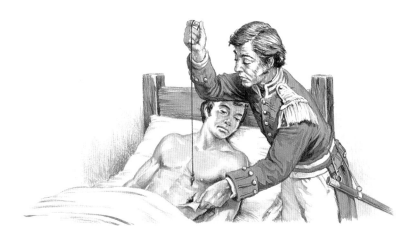

Figure A   Doctor Beaumont placing a piece of food into Alexis St Martin's stomach.

1 In the first experiment Beaumont was interested to find out if the stomach contained digestive juices all the time, even when no food was present.
   a) What conclusion could he draw from his observation?
   b) What prediction could he make from this observation?
2 What do you think Beaumont concluded from his second experiment?
3 The juices contain important chemicals made by the body. What are these called?
4 What did you think Beaumont concluded from his experiments with food on strings?
5 What do you think Beaumont concluded from his experiment on St Martin's meal?
6 Beaumont also investigated the action of the stomach juice outside the stomach. Why would he have kept the juice at body temperature?
7 If you were Alexis St Martin would you have allowed Dr Beaumont to carry out his investigation? Explain your reasons.

The food is churned up by the action of the muscles as they send peristaltic waves down the stomach walls at the rate of about three per minute. The food is prevented by a valve from leaving the stomach. When the food is broken down into a creamy liquid the valve opens, which allows the liquid food to pass through into the next part of the digestive system.

Duodenum, liver and pancreas

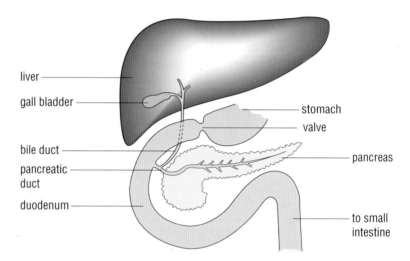

Figure 7.6   The duodenum, liver and pancreas.

The duodenum is a tube that connects the stomach to the small intestine. Two other tubes are connected to it. One tube carries a green liquid called bile from the gall bladder to mix with the food. Bile is made in the liver and contains chemicals that help break down fat into small droplets so that fat-digesting enzymes can work more easily. The second tube comes from an organ called the pancreas. This is a gland that produces a juice containing enzymes that digest proteins, fats and carbohydrates. The mixture of liquids from the stomach, liver and pancreas pass on into the small intestine.

Small intestine

The cells lining the wall of the small intestine make enzymes that complete the digestion of carbohydrates and proteins. Proteins are broken down into amino acids, carbohydrates are broken down into sugars, and fats are broken down into fatty acids and glycerol.

6 Where is bile made and what does it do?

7 What are proteins, fats and carbohydrates broken down into?

8 Where are the digested foods absorbed?

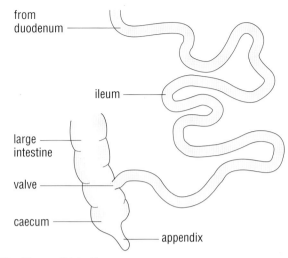

Figure 7.7   The small intestine.

All these small molecules are soluble and can pass through the wall of the small intestine. They are carried by the blood to all cells of the body.

Fate of undigested food

Indigestible parts of the food, such as cellulose, pass on through the small intestine to the large intestine and colon. Here water and some dissolved vitamins are absorbed and taken into the body. The remaining semi-solid substances form the faeces, which are stored in the rectum. The faeces are removed from the body through the anus perhaps once or twice a day in a process called egestion.

9 What happens to undigested food in the large intestine?

10 What happens in egestion?

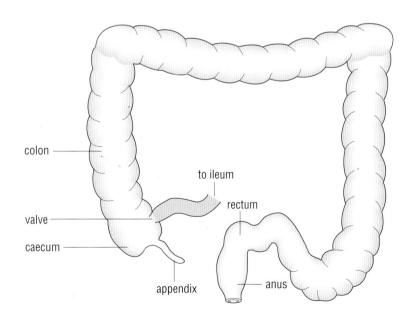

Figure 7.8   The large intestine and rectum.

11 What kind of enzyme is produced in
   a) the mouth and
   b) the stomach?

12 What kind of enzyme does bile help?

13 Where does bile come from?

14 Which organ of the digestive system produces all three kinds of enzyme?

15 Why do small droplets of fat get broken down by enzymes more quickly than large droplets?

Enzymes

An enzyme that digests carbohydrate is called a carbohydrase. An enzyme that digests protein is called a protease. An enzyme that digests fat is called a lipase.

Table 7.1 Enzymes.

Region of production	Kind of enzyme	Notes
Salivary glands in mouth	Carbohydrase	Enzyme is called salivary amylase
Gastric glands in stomach	Protease	Enzyme is called pepsin Hydrochloric acid is also made to help the enzyme work
Pancreas	Protease, carbohydrase, lipase	Enzymes enter the duodenum and mix with food and bile

◆ SUMMARY ◆

◆ There are four kinds of teeth. They are the incisors, canines, premolars and molars. They have special shapes for specific tasks (*see pages 104–105*).

◆ The purpose of digestion is to break down the food into substances that can be absorbed and used by the body (*see page 104*).

◆ Enzymes break down the large molecules in food into smaller molecules so that they can be absorbed by the body (*see page 105*).

◆ The food is moved along the gut by a wave of muscular contraction called peristalsis (*see page 108*).

◆ The food is digested by enzymes that are made in the salivary glands, the stomach wall, the pancreas and the wall of the small intestine (*see pages 107, 108–110, 112*).

◆ The liver produces bile, which helps in the digestion of fat (*see page 110*).

◆ Digested food is absorbed in the small intestine (*see page 110*).

◆ The undigested food has water removed from it in the large intestine and is then stored in the rectum before being released through the anus (*see page 111*).

End of chapter questions

1 Collect a copy of Figure 7.9 from your teacher and use the other diagrams in this chapter to label all the parts of the digestive system.

2 Describe the digestion of a chicken sandwich.

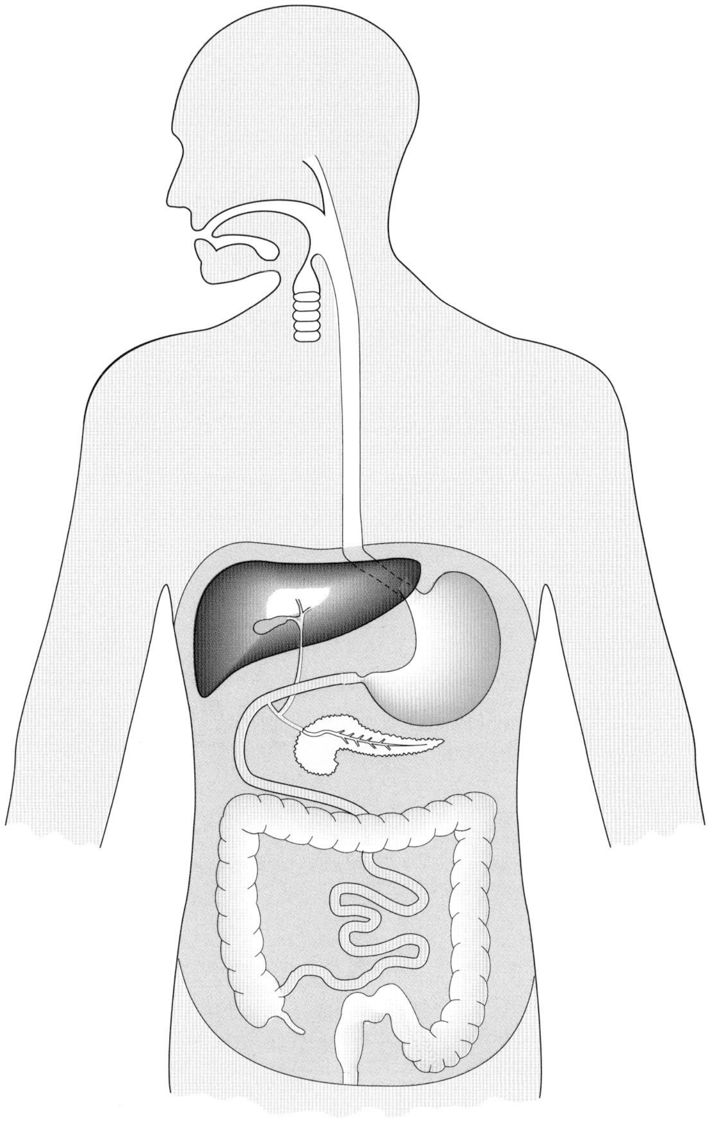

Figure 7.9 The digestive system.

8

Circulation and breathing

Circulation and breathing are very closely linked in the body. Breathing provides the means of taking in oxygen and releasing carbon dioxide. Circulation provides the means of transporting oxygen and carbon dioxide round the body. In this chapter we look at circulation and then breathing.

The heart

Movement of the blood is produced by the pumping action of the heart. The heart is divided down the middle into two halves. The right side receives deoxygenated blood (blood which has lost its oxygen) from the body and pumps it to the lungs. At the same time the left side receives oxygenated blood (blood rich in oxygen) from the lungs and pumps it to the body.

The two pumps in the heart and a simplified arrangement of the blood vessels are shown in Figure 8.1.

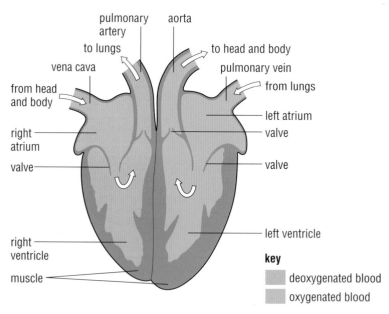

Figure 8.1 A simplified section through the heart.

1 Where does the pushing force come from to push the blood out of the heart?
2 What is the purpose of the heart valves?
3 Why do you think the walls of the left ventricle are thicker than the walls of the right ventricle?

Each side of the heart has two chambers. Blood flows from the veins (see page 116) into the upper chambers called the atria (*singular:* atrium). It passes from the atria into the lower chambers, the ventricles. The muscular walls of the ventricles relax as they fill up. When these muscular walls contract the blood is pumped into the arteries (see page 115). Valves between the atria and the ventricles stop the blood going backwards into the atria. Valves between the arteries (aorta and pulmonary artery) and the ventricles stop the blood from flowing backwards after it has been pumped out of the heart.

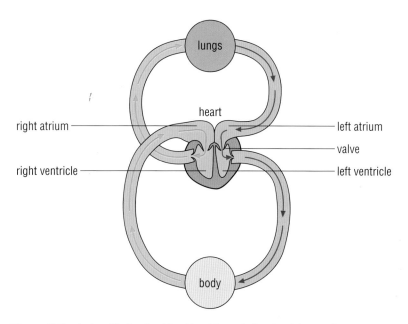

Figure 8.2 A simplified path of the blood through the circulatory system.

Blood vessels

Arteries

Blood vessels that take blood away from the heart are called arteries. The high pressure of blood pushes strongly on the thick, elastic artery walls. They stretch and shrink as the blood moves by. This movement of the artery wall makes a pulse. When an artery passes close to the skin the pulse can be felt and therefore used to count how fast the heart is beating.

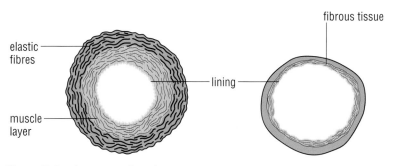

Figure 8.3 An artery and a vein.

4 Why do veins have valves?
5 Why do you think arteries function better with thick walls?

Veins

Blood vessels that bring blood towards the heart are called veins. The blood is not under such high pressure and so does not push as strongly on the vein walls. Veins have thinner walls than arteries and contain valves that stop the blood flowing backwards.

Capillaries

When an artery reaches an organ it splits into smaller and smaller vessels. The smallest blood vessels are called capillaries. A capillary wall is only one cell thick. Capillaries are spread throughout the organ so that all cells have blood passing close to them. Where the blood leaves an organ, capillaries join together to form larger and larger vessels until eventually they form veins.

What is in the blood?

About 45% of a drop of blood is made from cells. There are two kinds, red cells and white cells.

Red cells contain haemoglobin, which transports oxygen from the lungs to the other body cells. Haemoglobin allows the blood to carry 100 times more oxygen than the same amount of water. There are 500 red cells for every white cell.

White cells fight disease. They attack bacteria and produce chemicals to stop virus infections. White cells also gather at the site of a wound where the skin has been cut. They eat bacteria that try to enter. The white cells die in this process and their bodies collect to form pus in the wound.

The blood also carries platelets, which are fragments of cells. These collect in the capillaries at the site of a

6 Could you live without haemoglobin? Explain your answer.
7 Compare the tasks of red and white blood cells.

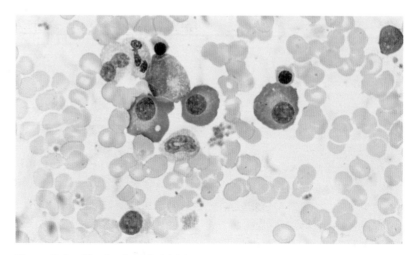

Figure 8.4 Blood cells and platelets.

wound and act to block the flow of blood. Platelets help the blood to form clots at the site of a wound. These clots stop blood leaking out of the wound.

About 55% of blood is a watery liquid called plasma. This contains digested foods, hormones such as adrenaline (see page 28), a waste product from the liver called urea and the carbon dioxide produced by all the body cells.

Moving oxygen to the cells

Once oxygen has entered the red blood cells it begins its journey inside the body. It starts by moving through the capillaries in the lungs. Capillaries are just one of three kinds of blood vessels found in the body (the other two are arteries and veins). They make a network of fine tubes in organs which provide a very large surface area between the blood and the tissues in the organs. This surface area allows a large amount of substances, such as oxygen and glucose, to pass between the blood and the tissues in a short amount of time. When the blood moves away from the lungs, it travels along a larger blood vessel called the pulmonary vein. The oxygenated blood is transported to the heart in the pulmonary vein, and is then circulated around the body.

Moving carbon dioxide to the lungs

Carbon dioxide is a product of aerobic respiration. It leaves the cells where it is produced and passes through the walls of the capillaries. It does not enter the red blood cells but stays in the plasma. It travels along veins which take it back to the right side of the heart. From here it enters the pulmonary artery and travels to the lungs. It escapes through the capillary walls into the air in the alveoli.

Moving glucose to the cells

Glucose contains the store of energy that is released during respiration. It reaches the cells in the following way. Glucose passes through the wall of the small intestine and into the capillaries. It does not enter the red blood cells but stays in the yellow watery part of the blood called the plasma. The glucose travels in the plasma along veins, which bring it to the heart. It enters the right side of the heart then passes to the lungs where the blood picks up oxygen. It then passes through the left side of the heart and into the aorta. From here it travels along arteries which take the glucose to the body organs.

8 How is the movement of oxygen in the body
   a) similar to and
   b) different from the movement of carbon dioxide?
9 How is the movement of glucose in the blood similar to the movement of carbon dioxide?

Studies on the circulatory system

Erasistratus (about 304–250 BC) was a Greek doctor who studied the circulatory system. He suggested that veins and arteries carried different substances. He thought that veins carried blood and arteries carried 'animal spirit'.

Galen (about AD130–200) was also a Greek doctor. He used the pulse of patients to help him to assess their sickness. He realised that the blood from one side of the heart got to the other side but he did not know how it happened. He thought there were tiny holes in the wall between the two sides of the heart. Galen also thought that the blood went backwards and forwards along the blood vessels. His ideas were held in high regard for over 1400 years.

Michael Servetus (1511–1553) was a Spanish doctor who traced the path of blood to and from the heart along the vein and artery that go to and from the lungs. He did not think that the blood went into the heart's muscular walls.

Fabricius ab Aquapendente (1537–1619) was a professor of surgery who discovered that the veins had valves in them. He taught the Englishman William Harvey (1578–1657) who became a doctor and went on to do further studies of the circulatory system. Fabricius's discovery of the valves gave Harvey a clue as to how the blood might flow. He followed up Fabricius's discovery by blocking an artery by tying a cord around it. He found that the side towards the heart swelled up because of the collecting blood. Next, he tied a cord around a vein. He found that the vein swelled on the side away from the heart.

Harvey also calculated the amount of blood that the heart pumped out in an hour. It was three times the weight of a man, yet the body did not increase in size. One explanation was that the heart made this amount of blood in an hour and another organ in the body destroyed it so the body did not increase in size. Harvey thought it impossible for the blood to be made and destroyed so quickly and so suggested that the blood must move around the body in only one direction. He published his ideas in a book in 1628 and was ridiculed by other doctors for challenging the ideas of Galen. Eventually the idea of the blood circulating round the body was accepted but Harvey could not explain how the blood got from the arteries to the veins.

Marcello Malpighi (1628–1694) was an Italian scientist who studied the wing of a bat under a microscope. He found that there was a connection between the arteries and veins in the wing. These were tiny vessels that could not be seen with the eye. These vessels were called capillaries and the blood could be seen flowing through them.

1 Who first described arteries and veins?
2 Who first began to doubt Galen's ideas?
3 How did Fabricius's discovery help Harvey?
4 If the blood flowed as Galen suggested what would Harvey have found when he tied off the artery and vein?
5 How did Harvey interpret his observations?
6 Why was Harvey's idea ridiculed?
7 How did Malpighi's work support Harvey's ideas?

Figure A   William Harvey at work.

A healthy heart

The heart may beat up to 2500 million times during a person's life. Its function is to push blood around the 100 000 km of blood vessels in the body. This push creates a blood pressure that drives the blood through the blood vessels. As the ventricles in the heart fill with blood the pressure in the blood vessels is reduced, but as the heart pumps it out along the arteries the blood pressure rises. The walls of the arteries are elastic and they stretch and contract with the blood pressure. In young people the artery walls are clear and their diameters are large enough to let the blood flow with ease. As the body ages the artery walls become less elastic.

The heart has its own blood vessels called the coronary arteries and veins. They transport blood to and from the heart muscle.

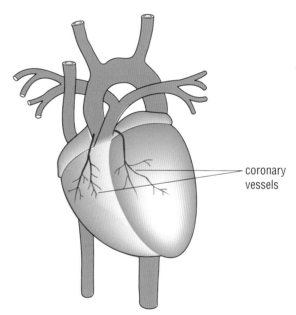

coronary vessels

Figure 8.5 The coronary blood vessels.

Fatty substances, such as cholesterol, stick to the walls of arteries. Calcium settles in the fatty layer and forms a raised patch called an atheroma. The blood then has less space to pass along the arteries and its pressure rises as it pushes through the narrower tubes. Other components of the blood, such as platelets, settle on the atheroma and make it larger. This may cause a blood clot which narrows the artery even more or can completely block it, causing a thrombosis. This means that the artery is unable to supply oxygen and other nutrients to the relevant organ. A thrombosis in a coronary artery causes a heart attack. A thrombosis in an artery in the brain causes a stroke.

The features that develop in the body that cause heart disease can be inherited. People whose relatives have suffered from heart disease should take special care to keep their heart and circulatory system healthy.

Keeping the heart healthy

The heart is made of muscle and like all muscles it needs exercise if it is to remain strong. The heart muscles are exercised when you take part in the activities in Table 2.1 (see page 29). Heart muscle contracts more quickly and more powerfully during exercise than it does at rest so that more blood can be pumped to your muscles. These muscles need more blood to provide extra oxygen while they work.

As we have seen, the blood supply to heart muscles can be reduced by fatty substances such as cholesterol in the blood. These substances are formed after the digestion of fatty foods. Some fatty substances are needed to keep the membranes of the cells healthy, but too much intake of fat leads to heart disease. A heart can be kept healthy by cutting down on the amount of fat in the diet. This may be achieved by cutting fat off meat, or eating fewer crisps and chips for example.

If large amounts of fat are eaten the fat is stored in the body. In time, a person who eats a diet high in fat will become obese. This puts extra strain on the heart as it tries to push the blood to the greatly enlarged body. The extra strain on the heart and the build up of fatty substances in the coronary artery can cause the heart muscle to fail and the person has a heart attack. Obesity can be avoided by eating a balanced diet (see page 99) and using the pyramid of food (see page 102) as a guide.

For discussion

How could a campaign for 'keeping your heart healthy' be carried out in your school? How could you assess if the campaign had been a success?

Care with exercise

When people decide to get fit, they may choose one of the activities from Table 2.1 page 29 and begin with great enthusiasm. However, they may experience a sprain or pains by trying to exercise too hard too early. The skeleton and muscles work together to provide movement.

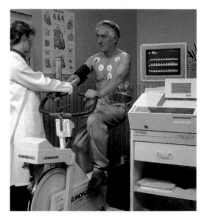

Figure 8.6 Pedalling an exercise bicycle makes the heart beat faster to provide blood for the leg muscles.

Someone who has not been active for a long time may need to build up their exercises gradually so that the muscles and joints can become adapted to the increased activity. If this is not done and someone receives an injury early on in their exercise programme they may decide not to continue, and they will become unfit again. It can help to be aware of how the skeleton and muscles work, and to think of them when an exercise programme is begun.

Respiratory system

In Chapter 7 we saw how food is broken down in the digestive system in readiness for transport to the cells. In this section we look at how the respiratory system provides a means of exchanging the respiratory gases – oxygen and carbon dioxide.

The function of the respiratory system is to provide a means of exchanging oxygen and carbon dioxide that meets the needs of the body, whether it is active or at rest. In humans the system is located in the head, neck and chest. It can be divided into three parts – the air passages and tubes, the pump that moves the air in and out of the system, and the respiratory surface. The terms respiration and breathing are often confused but they do have different meanings. Breathing just describes the movement of air in and out of the lungs. Respiration covers the whole process by which oxygen is taken into the body, transported to the cells and used in a reaction with glucose to release energy, with the production of water and carbon dioxide as waste products.

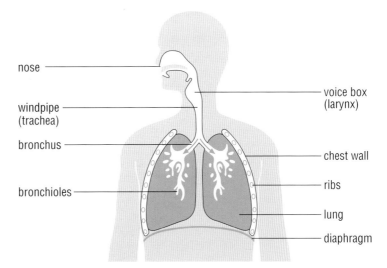

Figure 8.7   Respiratory system.

Air passages and tubes

Nose

Air normally enters the air passages through the nose. Hairs in the nose trap some of the dust particles that are carried on the air currents. The lining of the nose produces a watery liquid called mucus. This makes the air moist as it passes inwards, and also traps bacteria that are carried on the air currents. Blood vessels beneath the nasal lining release heat that warms the air before it passes into the lungs.

Windpipe

The windpipe or trachea is about 10 cm long and 1.5 cm wide. It is made from rings of cartilage, which is a fairly rigid substance. Each ring is in the shape of a 'C'. The inner lining of the windpipe has two types of cells. They are mucus-secreting cells and ciliated epithelial cells. Dust particles and bacteria are trapped in the mucus. The cilia beat backwards and forwards to move the mucus to the top of the windpipe where it enters the back of the mouth and is swallowed.

Bronchi and bronchioles

The windpipe divides into two smaller tubes called bronchi. (This is the name for more than one tube. A single tube is called a bronchus.) The two bronchi are also made of hoops of cartilage and have the same lining as the windpipe.

10 What structures hold the air passages open in the windpipe and bronchi?

11 Why is it more difficult to breathe during an asthmatic attack?

The bronchi divide up into many smaller tubes called bronchioles. These have a diameter of about 1 mm. The bronchioles divide many times. They have walls made of muscle but do not have hoops of cartilage. The wall muscles can make the bronchiole diameter narrower or wider.

Some people suffer from asthma. They may be allergic to certain proteins in food or to the proteins in dust that come from fur and feathers. The presence of these proteins in the air affects the muscles in the bronchioles, and the air passages in the bronchioles become narrower. This makes breathing very difficult. A person suffering an asthmatic attack can use an inhaler that releases chemicals to make the muscles relax to widen the bronchioles.

Air pump

The two parts of the air pump are the chest wall and the diaphragm. They surround the cavity in the chest. Most of the space inside the chest is taken up by the lungs. The outer surfaces of the lungs always lie close to the inside wall of the chest. The small space between the lungs and the chest wall is called the pleural cavity. The cavity contains a film of liquid that acts like a lubricating oil, helping the lung and chest wall surfaces to slide over each other during breathing.

12 Why is there a film of liquid in the pleural cavity?

Chest wall

This is made by the ribs and their muscles. Each rib is attached to the backbone by a joint that allows only a small amount of movement. The muscles between the ribs are called the internal and external intercostal muscles. The action of these muscles moves the ribs.

Diaphragm

This is a large sheet of muscle attached to the edges of the 10th pair of ribs and the backbone. It separates the chest cavity, which contains the lungs and heart, from the lower body cavity, which contains the stomach, intestines, liver, kidneys and female reproductive organs.

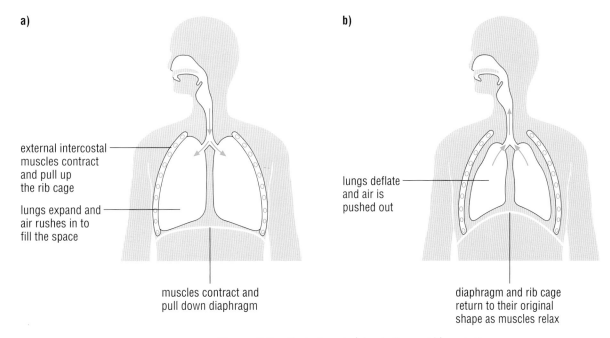

a)

external intercostal muscles contract and pull up the rib cage

lungs expand and air rushes in to fill the space

muscles contract and pull down diaphragm

b)

lungs deflate and air is pushed out

diaphragm and rib cage return to their original shape as muscles relax

Figure 8.8 Illustration of **a)** inspiration and **b)** expiration.

Breathing movements

There are two breathing movements – inspiration and expiration.

Inspiration

During inspiration the external intercostal muscles contract and the ribs move upwards and outwards. The muscles of the diaphragm contract, pulling it down into a flatter position. These actions increase the volume of the chest and reduce the pressure of air inside it. Therefore, air rushes in through the trachea and bronchi from outside the body. It is pushed in by the pressure of the air outside the body.

Expiration

The external intercostal muscles relax and the ribs fall back into their original position. Gravity is the main force that lowers the ribs and moves them inwards but the weak internal intercostal muscles may also help when they contract. The muscle fibres in the diaphragm relax and it rises to its dome-shaped position again. The organs below the diaphragm, which were pushed down when the diaphragm muscles contracted, now push upwards on the diaphragm. As the volume of the chest decreases, the pressure of the air inside it increases and air is pushed to the outside through the air passages.

Depth of breathing

The amount of air breathed in and out at rest is called the tidal volume and is about 500 cm^3 in humans. The maximum amount of air that can be breathed in and out is called the vital capacity. In human adults the vital capacity may reach 4000 cm^3.

Respiratory surface

At the end of each bronchiole is a very short tube called the alveolar duct. Bubble-like structures called alveoli open into this duct. Each alveolus has a moist lining, a thin wall and is supplied with tiny blood vessels called capillaries.

Oxygen from the inhaled air dissolves in the moist alveolar lining and moves by diffusion through the walls of the alveolus and the capillary next to it. The oxygen diffuses into the blood and enters the red blood cells (see page 116), which contain a dark red substance called haemoglobin. The oxygen then combines with the haemoglobin to make oxyhaemoglobin, which is bright

13 How does the action of the external intercostal and diaphragm muscles draw air up your nose?

14 How do the values of the tidal volume and vital capacity compare?

15 A resting person gets up and starts running. Describe two ways in which the person's breathing pattern changes.

16 Why should a person's breathing pattern change between resting and running?

red. Blood that has received oxygen from the air in the lungs is known as oxygenated blood.

Carbon dioxide is dissolved in the watery part of the blood called the plasma. It moves by diffusion through the capillary and alveolar walls and changes into a gas as it leaves the moist lining of the alveolus.

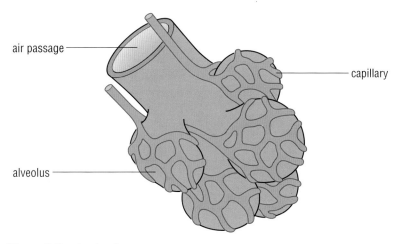

Figure 8.9   An alveolus.

Blood moves through the capillaries very quickly, so a large amount of oxygen and carbon dioxide can be exchanged in a short time.

The spongy structure of the lungs is produced by the 300 million alveoli which make a very large surface area through which the gases can be exchanged. It is like having the surface area of a tennis court wrapped up inside two footballs! If this surface area is reduced then health suffers.

17 How would thick-walled alveoli affect the exchange of the respiratory gases?

18 Compare the way the blood carries oxygen and carbon dioxide.

19 How do you think you would be affected if the surface area of your lungs was reduced?

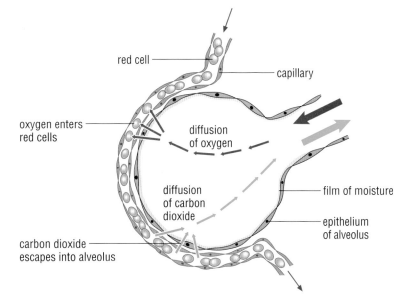

Figure 8.10   Diagram to show the direction of gaseous exchange.

Smoking and health

We have seen how the respiratory system works to provide us with an exchange of respiratory gases. An efficient exchange is needed for good health. When people smoke they damage their respiratory system and risk seriously damaging their health.

There are over a thousand different chemicals in cigarette smoke, including the highly addictive nicotine. These chemicals swirl around the air passages when a smoker inhales, and touch the air passage linings. In a healthy person, dust particles are trapped in mucus and moved up to the throat by the beating of microscopic hairs called cilia. The small amounts of dust and mucus are then swallowed. In a smoker's respiratory system the cilia stop beating owing to chemical damage by the smoke. More mucus is produced but instead of being carried up by the cilia it is coughed up by a jet of air as the lungs exhale strongly. This is a smoker's cough, and the amount of dirty mucus reaching the throat may be too much to swallow.

In time chronic bronchitis may develop. The lining of the bronchi becomes inflamed and open to infection from microorganisms. The inflammation of the air passages makes breathing more difficult and the smoker develops a permanent cough. The coughing causes the walls of some of the alveoli in the lungs to burst. When this happens the surface area of the lungs in contact with the air is reduced. This leads to a disease called emphysema.

For discussion

Should a person who becomes ill through having an unhealthy lifestyle receive the same amount of medical attention as someone who has an accident?

20 What is the function of a smoker's cough?

21 Why may chronic bronchitis lead to other diseases?

22 How does the reduced number of alveoli affect the exchange of oxygen and carbon dioxide?

23 Why does someone with emphysema breathe more rapidly than a healthy person?

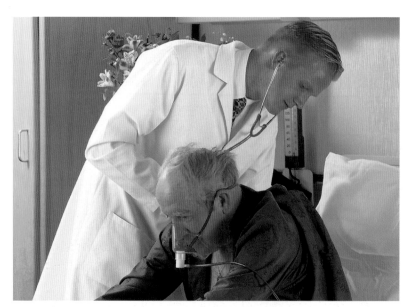

Figure 8.11 Effect of smoking on the respiratory system.

24 How are cancer cells different from normal cells in the lung tissue?

25 Why do cancer cells in an organ make the organ less efficient?

26 Why might the growth of cancer tumours in an organ have fatal results?

Some of the cells lining the air passages are killed by the chemicals in the smoke. They are replaced by cells below them as they divide and grow. Some of these cells may be damaged by the smoke too and as they divide they may form cancer cells. These cells replace the normal cells in the tissues around them but they do not perform the functions of the cells they replace. The cancer cells continue to divide and form a lump called a tumour. This may block the airway or break up and spread to other parts of the lung where more tumours can develop.

♦ SUMMARY ♦

- The heart contains two pumps for moving blood (*see page 114*).
- The three kinds of blood vessels are arteries, veins and capillaries (*see pages 115–116*).
- Blood is composed of plasma, cells and platelets (*see page 116*).
- Oxygen travels through the blood in the red blood cells (*see page 117*).
- Carbon dioxide travels through the blood in the plasma (*see page 117*).
- Glucose travels through the blood in the plasma (*see page 117*).
- Diet can affect the supply of blood to the heart (*see page 120*).
- Breathing is a process of gas exchange between the air and the lungs (*see page 121*).
- Breathing movements, inspiration and expiration, are caused by the movement of the chest wall and the diaphragm (*see page 124*).
- Smoking damages the bronchi and the alveoli and can cause bronchitis, emphysema and cancer (*see page 126*).

End of chapter question

1 Four people took their pulses (measured in beats per minute, on a portable heart monitor) at rest, straight after exercise, one minute after exercise, two minutes after exercise and three minutes after exercise. Here are their results.

Anwar 71, 110, 90, 79, 71
Belinda 74, 115, 89, 77, 73
Charles 73, 125, 115, 108, 91
Davina 53, 80, 71, 46, 64

a) Make a table of the results.
b) Plot a graph of the results.
c) What trend can you see in the results?
d) When did Anwar and Belinda's hearts beat at the same rate?
e) Anwar claims to be fitter than Charles. Do you think the results support his claim? Explain your answer.
f) Which result does not follow the trend? Explain why this may be so.

For discussion

Giorgio Baglivi (1668–1707) was an Italian doctor who believed that the body is just a machine. He matched scissors to teeth, bones to levers and lungs to bellows.

a) If he had been alive today, what might he have matched the brain to?

b) Was he right to think of the body as just a machine?

9 *Respiration*

The respiratory system was described in Chapter 8. The name 'respiratory system' suggests that it is the part of the body where respiration takes place. This is wrong because respiration takes place in every cell in the body. The respiratory system does, however, provide the means for all the cells to respire efficiently. It extracts oxygen from the air and releases carbon dioxide from the body.

Life processes occur in every cell. One example of a life process is the building up of proteins from amino acids produced by digestion (see page 93). The proteins are used to make or repair structures such as the cell membrane and enzymes, which help chemical reactions take place inside the cell. All life processes require energy. The energy is stored in food molecules and is released in respiration. In the human body the sugar glucose is the main source of energy. Most of it is formed from the digestion of starch. The energy in the sugar molecules is released when a chemical reaction takes place between sugar and oxygen. In this reaction carbon dioxide and water are produced. The chemical reaction for respiration can be written as a word equation:

glucose + oxygen → carbon + water   (with the release
dioxide   of energy)

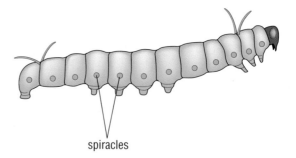

spiracles

Figure 9.1 Insects have a respiratory system made up of many air tubes which reach deep inside the body. You can see the openings of these tubes (called spiracles) along this insect's side.

1 What are the life processes that take place to show that an organism is alive?

2 Why are the spiracles of the diving beetle on its back? Look at page 84 to help you.

How the reactants reach the cells

3 Where does a body get its reactants for respiration from?

Glucose (a sugar) and oxygen are the reactants in the respiration process. Glucose enters the blood through the wall of the small intestine. It passes along a vein to the heart. From the heart it travels to the lungs and then back to the heart, leaving out the aorta (see page 115). From here it enters other arteries which take it to capillaries close to the cells in the organs of the body. The glucose passes from the blood to the cells by diffusion.

Oxygen enters the blood through the walls of the alveoli in the lung (see page 124). It passes into the red blood cells and combines with haemoglobin to make oxyhaemoglobin. The oxygen travels in the red blood cells along the pulmonary vein to the heart, then leaves the heart by the aorta. The blood travels to other arteries which take it to the capillaries close to the body cells. The oxygen breaks away from the haemoglobin molecules in the red blood cells and passes into the body cells by diffusion.

The products of respiration

Carbon dioxide passes out of the cells by diffusion and enters the plasma of the blood and dissolves in it. It travels in the blood to the lungs. When the carbon dioxide reaches the capillaries by the alveoli it diffuses out of the blood through the walls of the alveoli and into the lung air.

The water passes into the plasma in the blood. All chemical reactions of life processes take place in water. They work best at a certain concentration of water in the body. The brain controls the amount of water in the body so that the correct concentration is maintained. This means that if the body is short of water, the water released in respiration will be retained. If there is too much water in the body it will be released through the kidneys. Even if the body needs to retain water by reducing urine production it still loses water in other ways: through sweating to prevent the body temperature rising too high, through evaporation from the moist lining of the respiratory system, and in the faeces released by the digestive system.

4 Does a person sweat at the same rate in hot and cold conditions? Explain your answer.

5 Some people have the same amount of drinks in hot and cold weather. When are they likely to produce the most urine? Explain your answer.

Most of the energy released in respiration is used in life processes but some is released as heat. In mammals and birds life processes work within a small range of temperatures. The heat released by respiration is used to keep the body temperature within this range. If too much heat is produced, as in vigorous exercise, the heat is passed to the skin by the blood and is lost. Some heat is lost by radiation but most is lost by causing sweat to evaporate.

Figure 9.2   The ice that has formed here is from exhaled water vapour.

Testing for carbon dioxide

In exhaled air

Exhaled air can be tested for carbon dioxide by passing it through limewater. If carbon dioxide is present it reacts with the calcium hydroxide dissolved in the water to produce insoluble calcium carbonate. This makes the water turn white or milky.

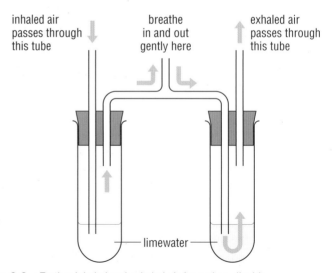

Figure 9.3   Testing inhaled and exhaled air for carbon dioxide.

6 What would you expect to happen in tube A if the soda lime did not absorb all the carbon dioxide in the air?

7 Does sealing the bell jar to the glass plate threaten to suffocate the animal? Explain your answer.

8 What changes would you expect to see in the apparatus if the animal produced carbon dioxide?

Production by animals

The apparatus in Figure 9.4 can be used to test animals for carbon dioxide production.

Air is drawn through the apparatus by a filter pump. The soda lime absorbs any carbon dioxide in the air before the air reaches the animal. The limewater in tube A is to check that all the carbon dioxide in the air has been removed. The bell jar is sealed to the glass plate with vaseline so that air cannot reach the animal without passing through the soda lime. The limewater in tube B is used to check for carbon dioxide in the air leaving the bell jar.

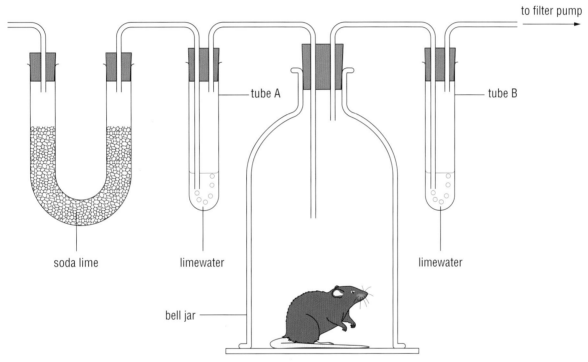

Figure 9.4 Testing animals for carbon dioxide production.

9 If someone connected the air pump to the other end of the apparatus by mistake, what do you think might happen?

Production by plants

Plants, like all living things, respire. They also make their own food by photosynthesis (see Chapter 11) and need carbon dioxide for this. Plants make food in the light and so in the daytime carbon dioxide in the air around them will be taken in. To test for carbon dioxide production the plant must therefore be kept in the dark. Figure 9.5 shows how a bell jar can be covered in black polythene or paper to prevent light from reaching the plant.

Seeds do not photosynthesise, so they can be tested for carbon dioxide without enclosing them in opaque material. As a seed germinates, the tiny plant it contains uses food stored in the seed to grow. The germinating seeds can be checked for carbon dioxide production by setting up the apparatus shown in Figure 1.12 page 18.

Hydrogencarbonate indicator can be used to test for carbon dioxide. If carbon dioxide is produced, the indicator changes from orange-red to yellow.

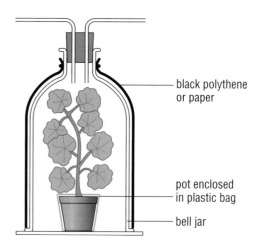

black polythene or paper

pot enclosed in plastic bag

bell jar

Figure 9.5

Respiration – a summary

For respiration to take place, oxygen and a source of energy (glucose) is required. During respiration the source of energy is used up. Energy is released, and some of it is in the form of heat. Carbon dioxide and water are also produced.

Comparing combustion

A burning candle is a common example of combustion. It can be used to compare combustion with respiration. The candle wax is the energy store (fuel) and during burning energy is released as heat and light. Two investigations are needed to show that combustion is very similar to respiration.

The use of oxygen

If a beaker is placed over a burning candle, the candle will burn for a while and then go out. A change has taken place in the air that makes it incapable of letting things burn in it.

The test for oxygen is made by plunging a glowing piece of wood into the gas being tested. If the gas is oxygen, the wood bursts into flame. When air from around the burned-out candle is tested for oxygen, the glowing wood goes out. This indicates that oxygen is no longer present. The oxygen in the air under the beaker has been used up by the burning candle.

The production of water and carbon dioxide

10 How could you use the apparatus in Figure 9.6 to show that changes seen in the investigation were due to the burning candle and not to other substances in the air?

If a burning candle is put under a thistle funnel which is attached to the apparatus shown in Figure 9.6 and the suction pump is switched on, a liquid collects in the U-tube and the limewater turns cloudy.

When the liquid is tested with cobalt chloride paper, the paper turns from blue to pink. This shows that the liquid is water. The cloudiness in the limewater indicates that carbon dioxide has passed into it.

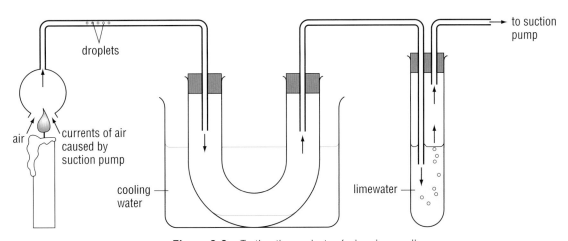

Figure 9.6   Testing the products of a burning candle.

Leaf structure and respiration

Plants do not make breathing movements to exchange oxygen and carbon dioxide. They rely on diffusion to move the gases in and out of their cells and in and out of their bodies. The leaves provide a plant with a huge surface area for capturing sunlight for photosynthesis. They also provide a huge surface area for diffusion to take place. However, the surfaces of the leaves are covered in wax to prevent water escaping and this also prevents the diffusion of the gases. Diffusion is still possible because the leaf surfaces have tiny holes in them called stomata (a single hole is called a stoma). These holes allow gases to pass in and out of the leaves. In plants such as trees which hold their leaves horizontally, the underside has the largest number of stomata. In plants such as grasses which hold their leaves vertically, the same number of holes is found on both sides of the leaf.

11 Why do you think that plants which hold their leaves horizontally have the largest number of holes (stomata) on the underside?

During the day when photosynthesis takes place, carbon dioxide is drawn into the leaf through the stomata by diffusion. Oxygen is not drawn in because during photosynthesis the plant makes more oxygen than it needs for its own respiration, and releases the excess through the stomata. During the night when only respiration occurs, the plant draws in oxygen from the air and releases carbon dioxide.

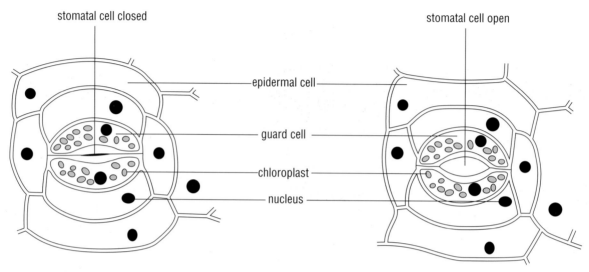

Figure 9.7 Stomata.

◆ SUMMARY ◆

◆ The word equation for respiration is glucose + oxygen → carbon dioxide + water with the release of energy (*see page 128*).
◆ Glucose and oxygen reach the cells by different routes (*see page 129*).
◆ Carbon dioxide and water, produced in respiration, pass into the plasma (*see page 129*).
◆ Limewater can be used to test for carbon dioxide (*see page 130*).
◆ A bell jar can be used to hold small animals in respiration experiments (*see page 131*).
◆ Plants respire (*see page 131*).
◆ Burning and respiration have similarities (*see page 132*).
◆ Respiratory gases pass in and out of plants by diffusion (*see page 133*).

End of chapter questions

A datalogger and light meter were set up to record the light intensity in a field of grass over a 24-hour period.

1 Draw a graph of how you would expect the light intensity to vary over this time.
A second datalogger was set up with a carbon dioxide probe to record the amount of carbon dioxide in a field over the same period of time.
2 Draw a graph of how you would expect the concentration of carbon dioxide to vary over this time.
3 Explain how the second graph relates to the first graph.

10 Flowering plants

The body of a flowering plant is divided into two parts – they are the shoot, which grows above the ground, and the root, which grows below it.

The shoot

Figure 10.1 Tomato fruits at different stages of development.

A shoot comprises several organs. They are the stem and its branches, the leaves, flowers and buds. In plants such as the tomato some flowers develop into organs called fruits while new flowers are still opening from buds.

The flower contains the reproductive parts of the plant. Many plants need insects to help them with the reproduction process, and they attract insects with large colourful petals, scent and nectar. The petals and the reproductive organs are protected in the flower bud by small leaf-like structures called sepals. The sepals usually fall off when the bud opens, but in some plants they stay attached to the shoot even when the fruit forms. In the tomato plant the dried up sepals form the spidery structure on the stalk of the tomato.

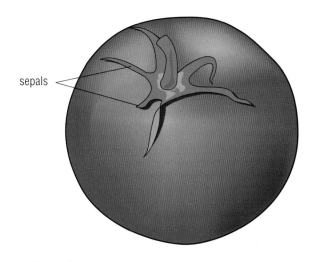

sepals

Figure 10.2 Sepals on a ripe tomato fruit.

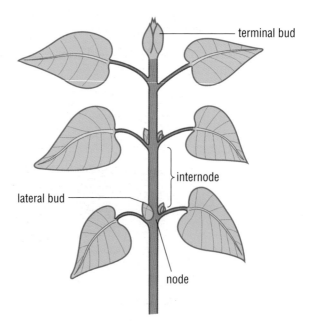

labels: terminal bud, internode, lateral bud, node

Figure 10.3

1 Look at any of the plants that there might be in your home or in school. Can the terminal bud, lateral buds, nodes and internodes be found easily in each plant? Do plants vary greatly in the structure of their shoots?

The major parts of the shoot are shown in Figure 10.3. The terminal bud is at the tip of the shoot. When it bursts open new growth is produced which makes the shoot longer. The lateral buds are on the sides of the shoots. When they burst open new growth produces side branches. Each lateral bud forms just above the point where a leaf grows out of the stem. The region where the leaf and bud is found is called a node. The gap between two nodes is called an internode.

The root

The root is not comprised of several organs like the shoot. It is made from many roots which spread out from under the shoot. The roots form a root system. There are two kinds of root system – the tap and fibrous root systems.

The tap root system, as seen in the carrot, has a thick central root, which grows deep into the soil and has small lateral roots growing from it. The fibrous root system, as seen in grass, is made from many small, thin roots which form a network in the soil.

2 Which type of roots – tap or fibrous – do you think are the easiest to pull up? Explain your answer.

In some plants, such as the yam, the root develops an organ called a tuber. This is a swollen region of the root in which the plant stores food.

Figure 10.4 These villagers have been gathering yams.

Transport tubes

The cells in plants and animals form groups. Groups of similar cells are called tissues. In plants two tissues of cells form tubes to transport food and water.

Water-conducting tissue

Water moves through the plant in xylem tissue. This tissue is made from xylem cells which die and form hollow tubes called xylem vessels (see Figure 10.5).

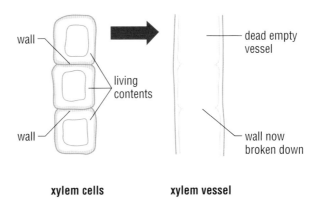

Figure 10.5 How a xylem vessel is made.

Water is needed in the leaf as a raw material for making food.

Food-conducting tissue

There is a second tissue which forms tubes – this is called phloem tissue. The tubes are made of living cells which transport the food made in the leaf to other parts of the plant.

3 How is xylem tissue different from phloem tissue?

The function of the root

The root has two major functions. It holds the plant in the ground and prevents it being blown away or blown over in a strong wind. The root also takes up water and minerals from the soil to help the plant make food and grow. It uses root hairs near the root tip to do this (see page 157). The water passes up the root in the xylem tissue. Food from the leaves passes through the phloem tissue to the root tips to help the tips grow and produce more root hairs.

Some roots sprout from the side of the stem – these are called adventitious roots. They help a weak stem hold onto a support. In ivy the adventitious roots grow into the bark of the tree that they are using as a support, to help the plant grow upwards.

4 How do the cells at the root tip depend on
  a) xylem and
  b) phloem for their survival?

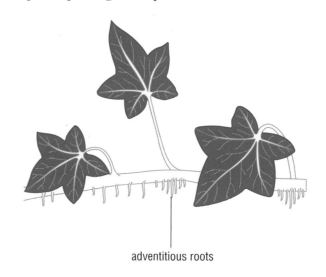

adventitious roots

Figure 10.6 Ivy plants have adventitious roots.

The function of the stem

The stem is the structure which provides support to the other organs of the shoot. It also contains a transport system between the root and all parts of the shoot. The stem holds up the leaves into the air and sunlight so they can receive carbon dioxide and light energy to make food. It holds up the flowers so that they can be better seen by insects or blown by the wind to help with pollination (see pages 163–165). Plants which disperse their seeds by the wind (see page 171) are helped if the stems are tall. This increases the distance the seeds must fall and increases the chance of them being blown away by the wind.

Water and minerals pass through the xylem tissue to all parts of the shoot but large amounts go to the leaves where they are used to make food. Phloem tissue moves food from all parts of the shoot and down to the root.

The xylem and phloem tissues form structures in the stem called vascular bundles. If you eat celery you have already met vascular bundles. They form the fibres which sometimes stick between your teeth!

5 In what ways are the functions of the root and the shoot
  a) similar,
  b) different?

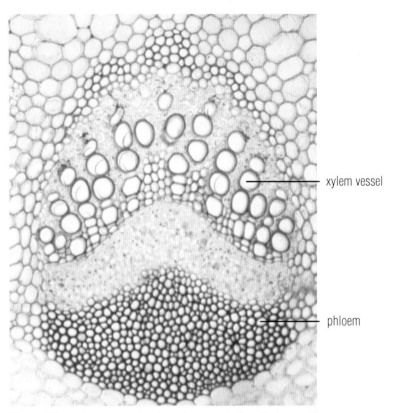

xylem vessel

phloem

6 Which tubes are wider – xylem or phloem?

Figure 10.7 A cross section through a vascular bundle in a sunflower stem.

The function of the leaf

The leaf has two vital functions. It makes food using the process of photosynthesis (see Chapter 11), and it helps to draw water through the plant from the roots.

Water from the roots

The root pushes water up a plant a little way. If a low branch on a tree is removed in spring, water may ooze from the cut owing to the root pushing it upwards. The power of the root to push up water can also be seen if a pot plant stem is cut near the soil surface and a glass tube is attached to it. When a small amount of water is added to the tube and it is left for a while the water level will be seen to rise a little.

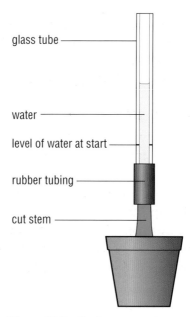

glass tube ————

water ————

level of water at start ————

rubber tubing ————

cut stem ————

Figure 10.8 Root pressure.

However, the power of the root to push water up the stem is not great. The water reaches all parts of the stem due to the action of the leaves.

Looking inside a leaf

If you look at a cross-section of a leaf under the microscope you will see that the cells form a number of tissues. The upper and lower surfaces are made from a layer one cell thick. This is called the epidermis. On the outer surface of the epidermal cells is a layer of wax, which prevents water passing in or out of the leaf. On the lower side of the leaf, holes called stomata may be seen (see page 134).

Sandwiched between the upper and lower epidermis are two more tissues. The upper tissue is called palisade tissue, and its cells are mainly involved with making food. Below the palisade tissue is the spongy mesophyll. The cells in this tissue also make food, but they also provide a surface for the evaporation of water.

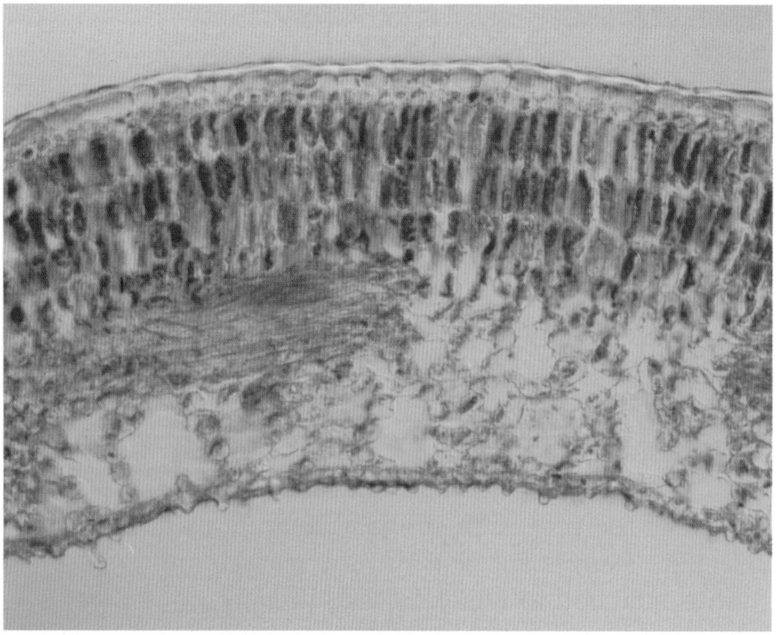

Figure 10.9 Cross section of a leaf. The cells in the palisade tissue are tightly packed while the cells in the spongy mesophyll have some air spaces between them.

7 a) Name the tissues labelled
   A, B and C in the section of
   this leaf.
   b) What is X?

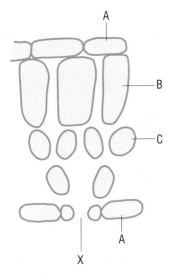

Figure 10.10

8 Describe the passage of a
water molecule from the soil,
up the transpiration stream to
mixing with other air particles
as water vapour.

9 a) How does temperature
   affect the evaporation of
   water in a dish?
   b) How do you think
   temperature will affect
   transpiration in a plant?

10 a) If washing is pegged
   outside to dry, will it dry
   quicker in still or windy
   conditions?
   b) How do you think windy
   conditions will affect the
   flow of the transpiration
   stream?

11 Humid air contains a large
amount of water vapour. This
makes it more difficult for water
particles to evaporate from a
dish of water. Will humid
conditions speed up or slow
down the rate of transpiration?

The veins in a leaf appear as circles or ovals in cross-section. They contain vascular bundles made up of xylem tissue, which carries water to the leaf, and phloem, which carries food away.

How water moves through a leaf

When water evaporates from cells in the spongy mesophyll layer, water vapour forms. If there is less water vapour outside the leaf than inside it, the water vapour will diffuse out through the stomata. This makes the spongy mesophyll cells short of water, and they take more from the xylem tissue in the veins. The water lost in the veins is replaced by water passing up the xylem tissue in the stem and root. The process in which plants lose water from their leaves is called transpiration, and the movement of water from the roots through the stem to the leaves is called the transpiration stream.

The release of water by transpiration can be shown by placing a clear plastic bag around the shoot of a pot plant as shown in Figure 10.11. The liquid inside the bag can be tested with cobalt chloride paper. If the paper turns pink the liquid is water.

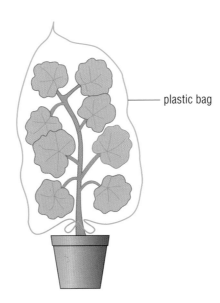

plastic bag

Figure 10.11 Demonstrating transpiration.

12 Look at Figure 10.11. How could you perform an experiment to show that
the amount of water collected was due to the leaves and not the stem?

Seed leaves

In a seed (see Chapter 12) there is a tiny plant waiting to grow. It has either one or two simple leaves called cotyledons. Plants with one seed leaf are called moncotyledons and plants with two seed leaves are called dicotyledons. When a monocotyledon grows from a seed it produces leaves which have parallel veins. When a dicotyledon grows from a seed it produces leaves which have a branching network of veins. By looking at the leaves of a plant you can tell how many seed leaves it had, and to which group of flowering plants it belongs.

1 Look at the plants around your home and school. Are they monocotyledons or dicotyledons?

Figure A   The banana leaf is a monocotyledon.

Figure B   The fig leaf is a dicotyledon.

The parts of a flower

The flower contains the reproductive parts of the plant. Most flowers have both male and female reproductive parts, as Figure 10.12 shows.

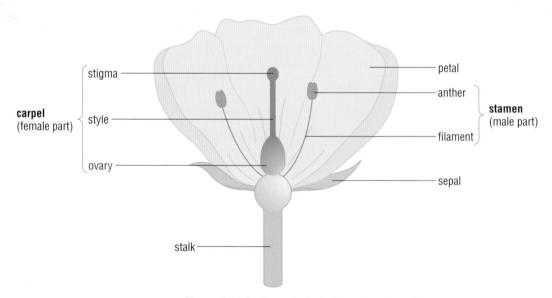

Figure 10.12   Parts of a typical insect-pollinated flower.

The sepal is a small tough, leaf-like structure. When the flower is in bud, a group of sepals lay over each other like tiles on a roof to protect it. The sepals form a ring called the calyx.

Petals are found in plants that use insects to pollinate their flowers (see pages 163–165). They are a large and colourful part of the flower. Some petals produce scent, and the colour and the scent attract insects to the flower. The petals form a ring called the corolla. The petals in the corolla may form a circle or a tube.

Inside the corolla are the stamens. They are the male part of the flower. Each stamen has two parts – the stalk, called the filament, and the pollen-producing organ called the anther. Inside the ring of stamens is the female part of the flower, which is made up from one or more carpels which may group together to form a pistil. Each carpel has a pollen-receiving surface called a stigma. Beneath the stigma is the style. It is connected to the ovary, which contains one or more ovules.

13 Imagine that you are watching a flower bud burst open. In which order will you see the parts of the flower?

Figure 10.13 Petals forming a circle.

Figure 10.14 Petals forming a tube.

Fruits

After flowers have been pollinated and fertilisation has taken place in the ovary (see pages 168–169) fruits develop.

Types of fruit

A fruit forms from the parts of the flower that continue to grow after fertilisation. There are two main types of fruit – dry fruits and succulent fruits.

Dry fruits have a wide variety of forms. They may form pods, such as those holding peas and beans, they may be woody nuts, such as acorns or hazelnuts, or grains like the fruits of wheat, oats and grasses.

14 What are the differences between dry friuts and succulent fruits?

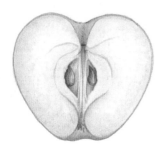

Figure 10.16 A peach (succulent fruit) and an apple (false fruit).

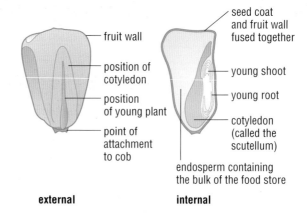

external   internal

Figure 10.15 Parts of a cereal grain.

Succulent fruits have a soft fleshy part. They may have a seed inside a woody skin which forms a 'stone' in the fruit, as in the cherry and peach. Many succulent fruits do not have a stone but contain a large number of smaller seeds, as in the tomato and orange.

Some fruits, such as apples, are called false fruits because their fleshy part does not grow from part of the flower but from the receptacle (the top of the flower stalk) on which the flower grows.

◆ SUMMARY ◆

- ◆ The shoot comprises the stem, branches, leaves, flowers and buds (*see page 135*).
- ◆ The flower contains the reproductive organs of the plant (*see page 135*).
- ◆ There are two kinds of root system – the tap and fibrous root systems (*see page 136*).
- ◆ Xylem is a water-conducting tissue (*see page 137*).
- ◆ Phloem is a food-conducting tissue (*see page 137*).
- ◆ The root holds the plant in the ground and takes up water and minerals (*see page 138*).
- ◆ The stem provides support and transports water, minerals and food (*see page 138*).
- ◆ The leaf makes food and draws water through the plant (*see page 139*).
- ◆ The root pushes water a little way up the plant (*see page 139*).
- ◆ The leaf is made from several tissues of cells (*see page 140*).
- ◆ The process in which a plant loses water from its leaves is called transpiration (*see page 141*).
- ◆ The main features of a flower are the sepals, petals, stamens and carpels. (*see page 142*).
- ◆ The stamen is the male part of the flower and is composed of the anther and filament (*see page 143*).
- ◆ The carpel is the female part of the flower and is composed of the stigma, style and ovary (*see page 143*).
- ◆ There are two main kinds of fruit – dry fruits and succulent fruits (*see pages 143–144*).

End of chapter question

1 Examine a plant and use the information in this chapter to describe it in as much detail as you can.

11 Photosynthesis

How experiments build up information

Scientific processes are not usually understood by a single activity or even one repeated several times for checking. Processes are worked out over many years by a large number of different experiments that require different apparatus and different techniques. They may include making observations, thinking up new ideas and making models to test ideas. The activities form part of a line of research that may go back many years. The results of each experiment may contribute something to our understanding of how a process works. Eventually the results of a large number of different activities may show how the process works. In the following pages a series of experiments are presented as very simple examples of how their results contributed to our understanding of how plants make food.

If you become a scientist you will use some of the features you read about here, such as looking at the work of others or learning a technique to use in your experiments, in addition to making investigations following the scientific method.

The willow tree experiment

In the 17th Century Joannes Baptista van Helmont (1580–1644) performed an experiment on a willow tree. He was interested in what made it grow. At that time scientists believed that everything was made from four 'elements': air, water, fire and earth. Van Helmont believed that water was the most basic 'element' in the universe and that everything was made from it. He set up his experiment by weighing a willow sapling and the soil it was to grow in. Then he planted the sapling in the soil and provided it with nothing but water for the next 5 years. At the end of his experiment he found that the tree had increased in mass by 73 kilograms but the soil had decreased in mass by only about 60 grams. He concluded that the increase in mass was due to the water the plant had received.

1 How fair was van Helmont's experiment? Explain your answer.
2 Did the result of the experiment support van Helmont's beliefs? Explain your answer.
3 If you were to repeat van Helmont's experiment how would you improve it and what table would you construct for recording your results?

Figure 11.1 Watering a willow tree.

If we were to summarise his conclusion it could look like this:

$$water \rightarrow mass\ of\ plant$$

Revising the work so far

As plants are food for animals the simple equation could be rewritten as:

$$water \rightarrow food\ in\ the\ plant$$

Moving on

The idea of food in the plant could then be investigated. A reasonable place to start could be with a plant part that is used as food – the potato.

Examining a potato with a microscope

If a small slice of potato is examined under the microscope the cells are found to contain colourless grains. When dilute iodine solution is added to the potato slice the grains turn blue–black. This test shows that the grains are made of starch.

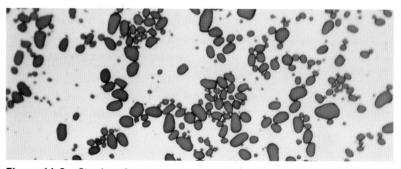

Figure 11.2 Starch grains.

Moving on

Having established that plant tubers such as the potato contain starch it may then be reasonable to try and find out if other parts of the plant contain starch. As the leaves are a major feature of most plants the search for starch in leaves would be the next task.

Testing a leaf for starch

Iodine does not produce a colour change when it is placed on a leaf because the cell walls will not allow the iodine into the cells and the green pigment masks any colour change. However, the work of others has shown that a leaf can be tested for starch if it is first treated with boiling water and ethanol. The boiling water makes it easier for liquids to leave and enter the plant cells and the ethanol removes the green pigment, chlorophyll, from the leaf and makes the leaf crisp.

If the leaves of a geranium that has been growing on a windowsill or in a greenhouse are tested, they will be found to contain starch.

Revising the work so far

Starch belongs to a nutrient group called carbohydrates, so, perhaps the simple equation could be altered to:

$$water \rightarrow carbohydrate\ (starch)\ in\ the\ plant$$

Moving on

Stephen Hales (1677–1761) discovered that 'a portion of air' helped a plant to survive, and Jan Ingenhousz (1730–1799) showed that green plants take up carbon dioxide from the air when they are put in the light. It was also known that water contains only the elements hydrogen and oxygen while carbohydrates contain carbon, hydrogen and oxygen. All this information led to a review of van Helmont's idea that only water was needed to produce the carbohydrate. The review began by considering what else was around the plant apart from water. It was known from van Helmont's work that the soil contributed only a very small amount to the increased mass of the plant. The only other material coming into contact with the plant was the air. Ingenhousz's work suggested that the carbon dioxide in the air was important. This idea can be tested in the laboratory.

4 What was the purpose of putting the leaf
   a) in boiling water and
   b) in ethanol?

Destarching a plant

If you want to see whether starch has been made you have to start with a plant that does not have starch. If a plant that has leaves containing starch is left in darkness for 2 or 3 days, then tested again, it will be found that the leaves are starch-free. The plant is described as a destarched plant. It can be used to test for the effect of carbon dioxide.

Investigating the effect of carbon dioxide on starch production

Soda lime is a substance that absorbs carbon dioxide and takes it out of the air. Sodium hydrogencarbonate solution is a liquid that releases carbon dioxide into the air.

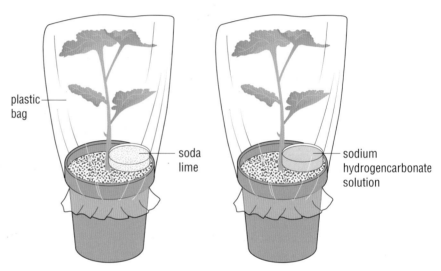

Figure 11.3 Plants set up to investigate the effect of carbon dioxide on starch production.

5 What does soda lime do to the air inside the plastic bag?

6 What does sodium hydrogencarbonate do to the air inside the plastic bag?

Two destarched plants were set up under transparent plastic bags that were sealed with an elastic band. Before covering the plants with the bags, a small dish of soda lime was added to one plant and a small dish of sodium hydrogencarbonate solution was added to the other. Both plants were left in daylight for a few hours before a leaf from each of them was tested for starch.

The leaf from the plant with the soda lime dish did not contain starch but the leaf from the plant with the sodium hydrogencarbonate did contain starch. This suggested that carbon dioxide is needed for starch production.

Revising the work so far

After reviewing the result of the effect of carbon dioxide on starch production the simple equation can be modified again to:

carbon dioxide + water → carbohydrate (starch) in a plant

Moving on

Joseph Priestley (1733–1804) studied how things burn. At that time scientists used the phlogiston theory to explain how things burned. They believed that when materials such as wood burned they lost a substance called phlogiston. When a candle burned in a closed volume of air, such as the air in a bell jar, they believed that the candle eventually went out because the air had become filled with phlogiston. It had become phlogisticated.

When Priestley put a plant in the air in which a candle had burned he found that later on a candle would burn in it again. He reasoned that the plant had taken the phlogiston out of the air and had made dephlogisticated air. Later, Ingenhousz re-examined Priestley's results and found that the phlogiston theory was wrong. The plants had in fact produced oxygen.

Water plants can be used to investigate the gases produced by plants because the gases escape from their surface in bubbles that can be easily seen and collected.

Investigating oxygen production in plants

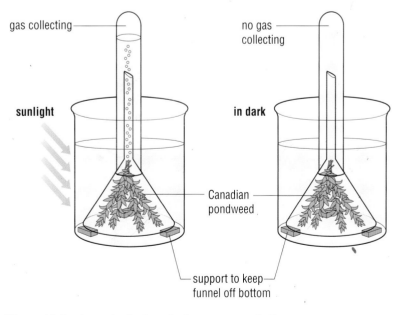

Figure 11.4 Apparatus for investigating oxygen production.

Two samples of Canadian pondweed were set up as shown in Figure 11.4. One was put in a sunny place and the other was kept in the dark. After about a week the amount of gas collected in each test-tube was examined. The plants in the dark had not produced any gas. The plants in the light had produced gas and when it was tested with a glowing splint the splint relighted, showing that the gas contained more oxygen than normal air.

Revising the work so far

From the result of this experiment the equation can be further modified to:

$$\text{carbon dioxide} + \text{water} \rightarrow \text{carbohydrate} + \text{oxygen}$$

Moving on

Having established that the carbohydrate starch is formed in leaves it may seem reasonable to find out what affects the presence of starch in leaves. What is it in the plant that allows the reaction to happen? Does the reaction happen all the time or only at certain times of the day or night?

Testing the effect of light on a destarched plant

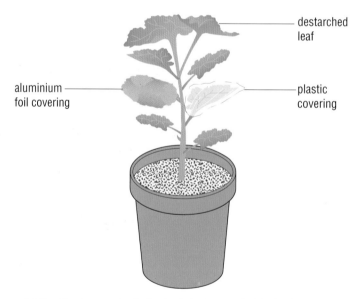

Figure 11.5 Two leaves of a destarched plant covered with plastic and aluminium.

Two leaves of a destarched plant were set up as shown in Figure 11.5 and left for over 4 hours in daylight. After that time they were removed and tested for the presence of starch. The leaf kept in the transparent plastic sheet contained starch. The leaf kept in the aluminium sheet did not contain any starch. This suggested that light is needed for starch to form in a leaf.

Revising the work so far

After reviewing the result of the effect of light on the leaf the equation can be modified to:

$$\text{carbon dioxide} + \text{water} \xrightarrow{\text{light}} \text{carbohydrate} + \text{oxygen}$$

Light provides the energy for the chemical reaction to take place. Some of the energy is stored as chemical energy in the carbohydrate.

Moving on

Having discovered a connection between the leaf, light and starch production it may seem reasonable to find out which part of the leaf is important. As most leaves are green it may be suggested that the green pigment, chlorophyll, which is found in chloroplasts of the leaf, is important. If it is lacking, starch should not be made. This hypothesis can be tested by using a variegated leaf, which has some cells that do not have chlorophyll thus making parts of the leaf appear white.

Investigating chlorophyll and starch production

A destarched variegated plant was left in daylight for over 4 hours. A leaf was then removed and tested for starch. The parts that were green contained starch but the parts that were white did not contain starch. This suggested that chlorophyll is needed for the leaf to produce starch.

Revising the work so far

After reviewing the result of the effect of chlorophyll on starch production, the equation can be modified to:

$$\text{carbon dioxide} + \text{water} \underset{\text{chlorophyll}}{\overset{\text{light}}{\longrightarrow}} \text{carbohydrate} + \text{oxygen}$$

Figure 11.6 A variegated pelargonium called Lady Plymouth.

Further experiments showed that the carbohydrate starch was built up in stages from subunits of a substance called glucose. The equation for starch production, or photosynthesis, is now written as:

$$\text{carbon dioxide + water} \xrightarrow[\text{chlorophyll}]{\text{light}} \text{glucose + oxygen}$$

7 Try to describe photosynthesis in your own words.

Fate of glucose

Glucose may be used to release energy in the process of respiration. The energy released is used for all life processes in plant cells. Glucose is also used to make many other molecules in the plant. It may be used to make cellulose for the cell walls or turned into fats for the cell membranes. Glucose may be changed into starch, which is an energy store for the plant, or made into sugars in fruits so that their sweet taste makes them attractive to animals (see page 171). Nitrogen and sulphur join with the elements in glucose to make amino acids and proteins.

Plant respiration

Plant cells need energy to drive their life processes. As in animals, this energy is released in respiration (see page 14):

$$\text{glucose + oxygen} \rightarrow \text{carbon dioxide + water} \quad \text{(with the release of energy)}$$

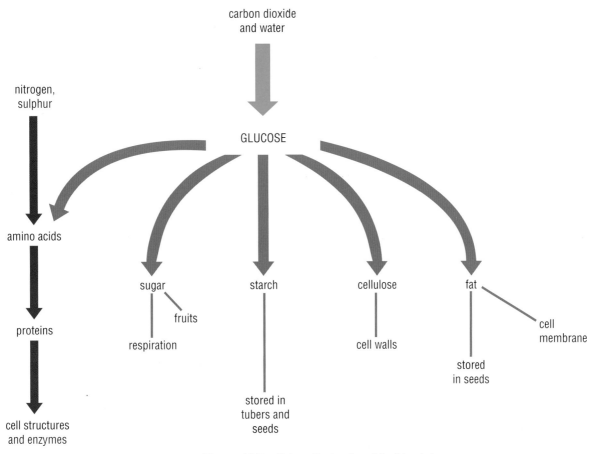

Figure 11.7 Schematic drawing of the fate of glucose.

8 What do plants take from the air and give to the air when they respire?

9 What do plants take from the air and give to the air during photosynthesis?

10 Compare the equations for photosynthesis and respiration.

11 How does the amount of
  a) carbon dioxide and
  b) oxygen vary around a plant over a 24-hour period? Explain your answer.

12 When will the amount of glucose in a leaf cell rise to a high concentration? Explain your answer.

13 Why does starch form?

14 When will the amount of starch in a leaf cell decrease? Explain why this happens.

Plants respire 24 hours a day. They take in oxygen and produce carbon dioxide. During daylight photosynthesis also takes place. In this reaction carbon dioxide is used up and oxygen is produced. In bright sunlight the speed at which plants produce oxygen is greater than the speed at which they use up oxygen in respiration.

Glucose and starch

Glucose is soluble in the cell sap. If the concentration of glucose in the cell sap is too high, too much water is drawn into the cell. When glucose is made in large quantities in the leaf cells it is converted into starch, which is insoluble and does not affect the way water enters or leaves the plant cells. When the concentration of glucose in the cell becomes low the starch is converted back into glucose.

Oxygen and carbon dioxide in the atmosphere

About 20% of the atmosphere is composed of oxygen and about 0.03% is composed of carbon dioxide. These two amounts remain the same from year to year. The reason they do not change is that the carbon dioxide produced by animals and plants in respiration is used up in photosynthesis, and the oxygen produced by the plants is used up by plants and animals in respiration.

Figure 11.8   Some of the oxygen that these deer are breathing has been produced by the trees around them.

15 Why do humans not suffocate at night when the plants around them cannot photosynthesise?

16 What effect will reducing the number of plants on the surface of our planet have on the animals?

Carbon cycle

The carbon dioxide taken into a plant is used to make glucose, which may be transported to a storage organ and converted into starch. If the storage organ is a potato, for example, it may be dug up out of the ground, cooked and eaten. The starch is broken down to glucose in digestion and taken into the blood. In the body the glucose may be used for respiration and the carbon is released as carbon dioxide. If too much high-energy food is being eaten the glucose may be converted into fat and the carbon remains in the body. When the body dies, microbes feed on it and break it down into simple substances. The microbes thus release the carbon back into the air, as carbon dioxide, when they respire.

17 Re-read the account of the carbon cycle and draw the paths that carbon can take.

18 Now add in the path that the carbon would take if the potato plant died.

19 Why is the path called the carbon cycle?

Plants and planets

The first plant-like organisms were algae. They lived in the sea. Today, huge numbers of algae live as plankton. This is the name given to the algae and tiny animals that live in the upper waters of the oceans. Most of the oxygen you breathe has been produced by algae.

About 400 million years ago, when the oxygen concentration of the atmosphere was about 1%, the first land plants developed. They were similar to horsetails and had relatively simple stuctures. Later, mosses, ferns and conifers developed. The first flowering plants developed 170 million years ago.

Humans developed in the past 2 million years and originally hunted animals for food or collected berries and roots to eat.

About 10 000 years ago humans discovered that more food could be obtained by planting seeds in the soil to grow crops. Today, the main food crops are wheat, barley, maize, millet, sorghum, rice, plantain, cassava and potato. The main growing regions for these crops are shown in Figure A below.

1 Which of the main food crops do you eat regularly?

2 Make a list of everything you eat for 2 days. Now remove all these main food crops and their products, such as popcorn (from maize), from your list.

   a) What foods would now remain in your diet?

   b) How important are these food crops to your diet? Explain your answer.

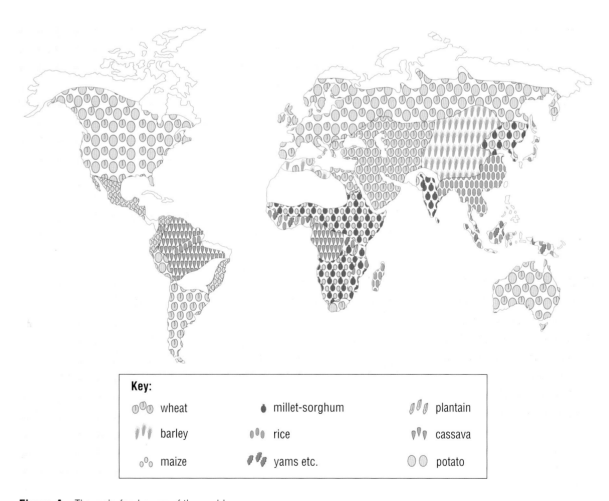

Key:

wheat	millet-sorghum	plantain
barley	rice	cassava
maize	yams etc.	potato

Figure A The main food crops of the world.

(continued)

In many places the natural vegetation has been destroyed to make room for people and farms, but in deserts plants are being used to develop small areas of land.

It has been suggested that if we wish to colonise another planet in the future, we may need to send specially developed plants there to spread across its surface in order to change the atmosphere into a breathable one.

Figure B   Reclaiming the desert.

20 Put the information about mineral salts and their uses by plants into a table. Include information about what happens if the mineral salt is missing.

21 What mineral might be missing if the leaves go yellow?

22 Why might a plant show poor growth?

Mineral salts

When chemists began studying plants they discovered that they contained a wide range of elements. With the exceptions of carbon, hydrogen and oxygen the plants obtained these elements from mineral salts in the soil.

The importance of each element was assessed by setting up experiments in which the plants received all the necessary mineral salts except for the one under investigation. From these studies it was found that:

- Nitrogen is taken in as nitrates and is needed to form proteins and chlorophyll. Without nitrogen the plant's leaves turn yellow and the plant shows poor growth.
- Phosphorus is taken in as phosphates and is needed to make chemicals for the transfer of energy in photosynthesis and respiration. Without phosphorus a plant shows poor growth.
- Potassium is taken in as potassium salt and helps the plant to make protein and chlorophyll. If it is lacking the leaves become yellow and grow abnormally.

Path of minerals through living things

When animals eat plants they take in the minerals and use them in their bodies. Some of the minerals are released in the solid and liquid wastes that animals produce. As bacteria feed on these wastes, the mineral salts are released back into the soil. The mineral salts are also released when the plants and animals die and microbes break down their bodies in the process of feeding. Plants, animals and their wastes are

23 Could you be a recycled dinosaur? Explain your answer.

biodegradable. This means they can be broken down into simple substances that can be used again to make new living organisms. These simple substances have been recycled since the beginning of life on Earth.

Lack of nitrogen

Lack of phosphorus

Lack of potassium

Figure 11.9 Plants showing mineral deficiency.

Water and minerals in the plant

Most plant roots have projections called root hairs. The tips of the root hairs grow out into the spaces between

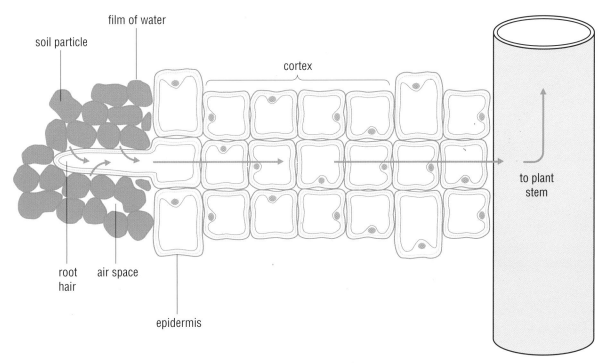

Figure 11.10 Schematic drawing of the movement of water and mineral salts in the root of a plant.

24 If a plant is over-watered all the spaces between the soil particles become filled with water. How does this water-logged soil affect
  a) the plant roots and
  b) the plant's growth?

the soil particles. There may be up to 500 root hairs in a square centimetre of root surface. They greatly increase the surface area of the root so that large quantities of water can pass through them into the plant. The water in the soil is drawn into the plant to replace the water that is lost through evaporation from the leaves. The plant does not have to use energy to take the water in.

Mineral salts are dissolved in the soil water. The plant has to use energy to take them in. This energy is provided by the root cells when they use oxygen in respiration. The roots get the oxygen from the air spaces between the soil particles.

Carnivorous plants

Some plants live in conditions where minerals are unavailable. They are therefore unable to take up minerals from the soil. These plants have developed a way of getting the elements they need. Their leaves have adapted to allow them to trap and kill animals. The most important element required is nitrogen.

Sundew grows in peaty bogs in the United Kingdom. The Venus fly trap grows in peaty bogs and waterlogged ground in the south-east of the United States. Pitcher plants (see Figure B) are found in tropical rainforests, in marshes in the United States and in some swamps in Australia.

The leaves of the sundew have long stalks and circular blades. The upper surface of the leaf blade is covered in hairs that secrete sticky drops of a liquid that contains protein-digesting enzymes. When an insect lands on the

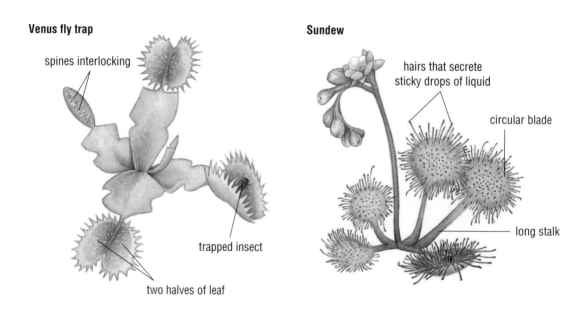

Venus fly trap

spines interlocking

trapped insect

two halves of leaf

Sundew

hairs that secrete sticky drops of liquid

circular blade

long stalk

Figure A

(continued)

leaf it sticks to the hairs and the enzymes digest its soft parts, leaving the hard parts to be blown away by the wind.

Each leaf of the Venus fly trap is divided into two halves that can spring together in 0.03 seconds. There are three hairs on each half of the leaf which act as triggers. If an insect lands on the leaf and touches them the trap is sprung. The spines on the edges of the leaf interlock and stop the insect escaping. A liquid is secreted from the leaf's surface which digests and absorbs the insect's body. In 24 hours the leaf opens again. After it has digested four insects the leaf dies and is replaced by a new one.

The rainforest pitcher plants are able to climb trees because they have cords, called tendrils, that stick out of their leaves. They curl around twigs and branches and give the pitcher plant support. The end of a tendril forms a hollow tube with a lid. This tube is called a pitcher and when it is fully grown the lid opens and water collects in it. The largest pitchers can hold up to 2 litres of water. There are glands at the mouth of the pitcher which produce nectar to attract insects. The inside walls of the pitcher are very smooth so that the insect loses its grip and falls into the water. Some pitcher plants also produce a drug in their nectar which makes the insect lose co-ordination and fall into the pitcher. There are hairs on the pitcher walls that point downwards to prevent the insect escaping. The insect drowns. As its body decays it releases nutrients into the water. These are absorbed by the walls of the pitcher. The pitcher plants that grow in the United States secrete enzymes and acids to digest the insects. In the Australian species, enzymes and bacteria break down the insects' bodies.

Pitcher plant

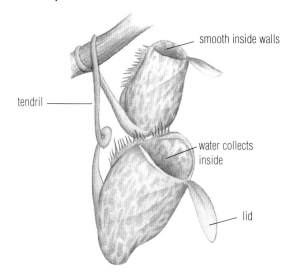

Figure B

1 What kind of conditions do not provide enough minerals for plants to grow well?
2 Why is nitrogen particularly important for plant growth?
3 How successful are the plant traps? Explain your answer.
4 What methods are used by carnivorous plants to break down an insect's body?

◆ SUMMARY ◆

- ◆ Iodine solution is used in the test for starch (*see page 146*).
- ◆ Boiling water and ethanol are used, with care, to remove chlorophyll from a leaf (*see page 147*).
- ◆ A plant is destarched by leaving it in the dark for 2 or 3 days (*see page 148*).
- ◆ Water and carbon dioxide are the raw materials of photosynthesis (*see page 149*).
- ◆ Light and chlorophyll are needed for a plant to photosynthesise (*see page 151*).
- ◆ Carbohydrate (glucose and starch) and oxygen are the products of photosynthesis (*see page 152*).
- ◆ Photosynthesis and respiration keep the levels of oxygen and carbon dioxide in the air constant (*see page 154*).
- ◆ Carbon passes from the air to a plant, then to an animal and finally a microbe releases it into the air again as it moves around the carbon cycle (*see page 154*).
- ◆ Mineral salts are needed for healthy plant growth (*see page 156*).
- ◆ Water and minerals enter the plant through the root hairs (*see page 157*).

End of chapter questions

How does a growing cucumber's weight change in a day? Large cucumbers appear to grow quickly. In this experiment a cucumber plant was placed close to a top-pan balance and one of its growing cucumbers was placed on the pan. The weight of the cucumber was measured every hour between 9.00 am and 4.00 pm. The weight was displayed in the graph in Figure 11.11.

1 What was the gain in weight over the 7-hour period?
2 Construct a table to display the increase in weight in each of the 7 hours.
3 When was the period of
  a) greatest and
  b) least growth?
4 If the cucumber plant had some of its leaves removed before the experiment, how would you expect its growth graph to compare with the graph in this experiment? Explain your answer.

For discussion

Using only the information in this chapter, suggest ways in which crop production could be improved.

The rainforests have been described as the world's lungs. What do you think this means?

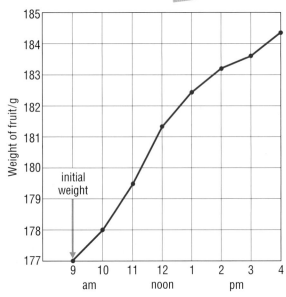

Figure 11.11

12

Seeds

The chances are that you have grown some plants from seed. If so, you have started the plants off on their life cycle. You may have let them grow until they produced flowers and then have seen them wither away and die. Alternatively you may still have a plant that you sowed from seed a few years ago. Plants have a variety of life cycles but they all start with a seed.

Life cycles

The life cycle of a flowering plant begins with a seed, which germinates and grows into a seedling. The seedling grows into a mature plant which produces flowers and later develops seeds. Many plants die after they have produced the seeds but some produce flowers and seeds for many years. This sequence of events is shown in Figure 12.1.

For discussion

Which plants that grow in your area produce flowers and seeds for many years?

Figure 12.1 Life cycle of a flowering plant.

The reproductive parts of the plant

Seeds are produced by reproduction. Many plants have flowers, which contain both the male and female reproductive parts. You can see them in an open flower in Figure 10.12 on page 142, and in Figure 12.2 below in a tubular flower.

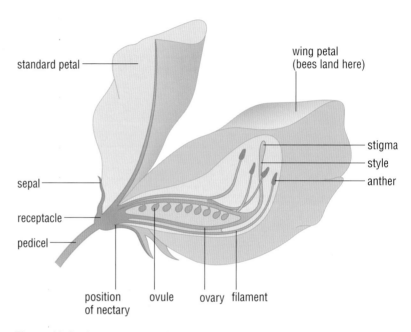

1 How can you tell the stigma from the stamens in the flower in Figure 12.2?

Figure 12.2   Insect-pollinated flower.

The male part of the flower is the stamen. It has two parts – the filament and the anther. The filament is a stalk which supports the anther and holds it in place in the flower. The anther produces pollen grains.

The female parts of the flower are the stigma, style, ovary and ovules. The stigma receives pollen grains. The style supports and holds up the stigma. The ovary forms a case which protects the ovules. The ovules change into seeds after fertilisation.

Pollen grains and pollination

When the pollen grains are fully formed in the anther it splits open to release them. Pollination occurs when pollen is transferred from an anther to a stigma. If the pollen goes from an anther to the stigma of the same flower or other flowers on the same plant the process is called self-pollination. Cross-pollination occurs if the pollen goes from the anther to the stigma of a flower on

Self-pollination

Cross-pollination

anther   stigma

Figure 12.3 Types of pollination in flowering plants.

2 What is the difference between self-pollination and cross-pollination?

another plant of the same species. Most plants produce flowers that have both male and female reproductive parts. They avoid self-pollination in two ways. Firstly, the anther can release the pollen before the stigma is ready to receive it, or secondly, the stigmas can be ready to receive pollen from other plants of the same species before their own anthers are ready to release their pollen.

There are two main ways in which the pollen grains are transferred from one flower to another for cross-pollination. They may be carried by insects or they may be carried by the wind. Pollen grains carried by insects may have a spiky surface which helps them stick to the hairs on the insect's body. Pollen grains carried by the wind are very small and light so that they can easily travel on air currents.

Insect- and wind-pollinated flowers

The flowers of insect-pollinated plants are different from the flowers of wind-pollinated plants.

Insect-pollinated flowers have a range of adaptations that attract insects. These adaptations include large colourful petals, scent and nectaries that produce a sugary liquid called nectar on which the insects feed.

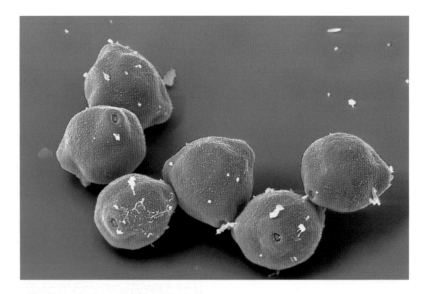

Figure 12.4 Highly-magnified views of pollen from a wind-pollinated plant (top) and from an insect-pollinated plant (bottom).

Some flowers produce more pollen than is needed for pollination and this may be taken as food by the pollinating insect. Many insect-pollinated plants, such as orchids, are adapted so that they attract just one species of insect. The shape and arrangement of the petals may allow one species of insect to enter a flower but keep out other species. The structure of the flowers encourages the transfer of pollen onto the insect and then onto the stigma of a plant of the same species. Short filaments keep the anthers inside the flower so that the insect can brush past them. The anthers of insect-pollinated flowers make a smaller amount of pollen than those of wind-pollinated flowers. Their stigma is often flat and held on a short style inside the flower so that the insect can easily land on it.

Figure 12.5   Insect pollination by a green metallic bee.

Wind-pollinated flowers are smaller than insect-pollinated flowers and do not show the adaptations shown above. They may have green petals and produce no nectar or scent. The flowers have long filaments which allow the anthers to sway outside the flower in the air currents. The anthers make a large amount of pollen and the stigma is a feathery structure which hangs outside the flower and forms a large surface area for catching pollen in the air.

3 Make a table to compare wind- and insect-pollinated plants.

4 Why does one method of pollination require much more pollen than the other method?

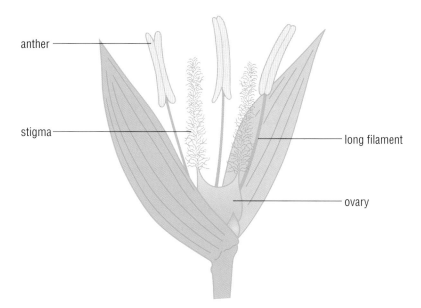

Figure 12.6   Wind-pollinated flower.

Bees and flowers

Karl von Frisch (1886–1982) was an Austrian zoologist who studied how bees communicate with each other. In 1973 he received a Nobel Prize for his work on animal behaviour.

The scent from a flower that has produced nectar travels through the air. It may stimulate the receptor cells of a honey bee and the insect flies towards it. As it gets closer, the bee also uses its eyes to find the flower. Its eyes are sensitive to ultraviolet light. This makes some of the pale markings we see in normal light stand out more distinctly to help the bee identify the flower. Some of the markings are lines running down the inside of the petal. They are called honey guides and direct the bee towards the nectar.

After landing on the flower the bee sticks its head between the stamens and probes the nectary with its mouth parts. While taking up the nectar it brushes past the anthers and pollen collects on the hairs of its back. When the bee has collected the nectar it flies on to the next flower and feeds again. Some of the pollen passes onto the stigma of the next flower.

The bee has stiff hairs on its front legs. Periodically it runs them through its body hair like a comb. This action collects the pollen off the bee's back and it is stored in structures called pollen baskets, which are made from hairs on its back legs.

1 What attracts the bee to the flower? Which sense organs does it use?
2 How do you think that Karl von Frisch gathered information about the honey bee's behaviour?
3 How does the behaviour of the dancing bee help a colony of plants which have come into flower?
4 How do you think the hive of bees survive the winter when there are no flowers to feed on?
5 Why are hives of bees kept in orchards?

Figure A   A bee in flight showing full pollen baskets.

When the bee swallows the nectar it collects in a cavity called the honey sac. The action of enzymes and the addition of other substances change the nectar into honey. After the bee has returned to its hive, it regurgitates the honey and passes it on to other bees working in the hive. They store it in the honeycomb. Also, the pollen is removed from the pollen baskets and stored.

The bee indicates the source of the nectar to the other bees in the hive by performing a dance on the honeycomb. The dance involves the bee moving in circles, waggling its abdomen and moving straight up and down on the vertical surface of the honeycomb. From this performance the other bees can tell the distance, direction and amount of nectar available and can set out to search for it.

For discussion
How useful are bees? Should we worry if there were fewer bees? Explain your conclusions.

Ununsual methods of pollination

In Britain most plants are either insect- or wind-pollinated. In different parts of the world there are variations in the way that flowers are pollinated. Here are just a few examples.

1 How could you arrange the unusual methods of pollination into groups?
2 Which flower acts as a trap?
3 Why do bat-pollinated flowers need to produce large amounts of nectar?
4 Which method carries the highest risk of failure?

Figure A The Bird of Paradise flower has stamens that form perches for birds. They pick up the pollen on their feet.

Figure B The century plant flowers contain large amounts of nectar for bats to drink. Each bat carries away the pollen on the fur on its head and neck.

Figure C A humming bird hovers in front of *Erythrina* sp. flowers while it probes into the flower with its beak to collect nectar. As it hovers it brushes its head on the stamens that are hanging outside the flower.

Figure D Honeysuckle flowers produce nectar at night to attract moths to pollinate them.

(continued)

Figure E   The cuckoo pint has male and female flowers on a short stem. There is a hood over the stem and the plant releases an unpleasant smell to attract small flies. The insects enter the hood and push through the downward-pointing hairs and over the female flowers. The stigmas of these flowers collect pollen from the insects. The hairs prevent the insects from leaving for a few days. During this time the male flowers make pollen. When they release it the hairs wither so that the insects can crawl over the male flowers, pick up the pollen and escape to take it to other cuckoo pint plants.

Figure F   *Rafflesia* is a parasitic flowering plant that lives on the roots of vines in the Malaysian rainforests. It produces a flower which is 91 centimetres across. This is the largest known flower of any plant. It is sometimes called the stinking corpse lily because of the smell of rotting meat that it produces to attract flies. There are separate male and female flowers and the flies they attract bring about pollination.

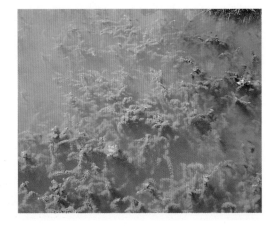

Figure G   Canadian pondweed produces male and female flowers on long stalks which let them reach the water surface. The male flower releases pollen onto the water and it floats away. Some of this pollen reaches the female flowers and pollination occurs.

Fertilisation

After a pollen grain has reached the surface of a stigma it breaks open and forms a pollen tube. The male gamete (cell) that has travelled in the pollen grain moves down this tube. The pollen tube grows down through the stigma and the style into the ovary (see Figure 12.7). In the ovary are ovules, each containing a female gamete (cell). When the tip of a pollen tube reaches an ovule the male gamete (cell) enters the ovule. It fuses with the female gamete (cell) in a process called fertilisation and a cell called a zygote is produced.

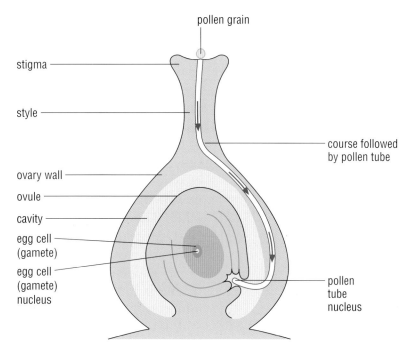

Figure 12.7 Fertilisation.

5 What is the difference between pollination and fertilisation?

6 Trace the path of a male gamete nucleus from the time it forms in a pollen grain in an anther until the time it enters an ovule.

After fertilisation

The zygote divides many times to produce a group of cells which form a tiny plant. Structures that later become the root and shoot are developed and a food store is laid down. While these changes are taking place inside the ovule the outer part of the ovule is forming a tough coat. When the changes are complete the ovule has become a seed (see Figure 12.8). As the seeds are forming other changes are taking place. The petals and stamens fall away. The sepals usually fall away too but sometimes, as in the tomato plant, they may stay in place. The stigma and style wither and the ovary changes into a fruit.

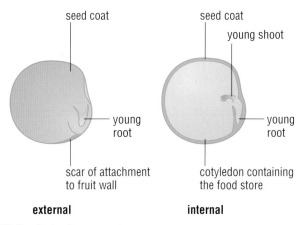

Figure 12.8 Parts of a pea seed.

Dispersing the fruits and seeds

A plant may produce many fruits. If they were all to fall to the ground around the plant the seeds inside them could eventually grow into new plants. There would be hundreds of new plants growing close together competing with each other for light, water and minerals in the soil, and so many would die. Overcrowding is prevented by fruit and seed dispersal. Plants use a range of ways to spread out their fruits and seeds so that when new plants grow they are not competing with each other. The disadvantage of dispersal is that seeds may land in unsuitable surroundings, in which they fail to grow. However, plants produce large numbers of seeds to be dispersed to increase the chance of some of them reaching suitable surroundings where they may grow into new plants.

A few plants, such as the oak tree of the northern hemisphere and the Brazil nut tree of the Amazonian rainforest, have fruits that simply drop to the ground. Some of the acorns from the oak tree are collected and stored by squirrels and mice some distance from the tree. The Brazil nut fruit has a tough outer coating which is opened by the agouti. This large rat-like mammal carries the seeds away and stores them. The squirrels, mice and agoutis return to their food stores to feed on the seeds, but they forget where they have stored all of the seeds. These seeds may eventually germinate and grow successfully into trees without competing with other seedlings or the parent tree.

Goose grass, burdock and agrimony have fruits with hooks on them. The hooks stick to the fur of passing mammals and they may be carried several kilometres before they are rubbed off and fall to the ground.

For discussion

How could water be used to disperse fruits of some plants? Explain your answer.

How would the fruit have to be adapted to survive?

Figure 12.9 Animal-dispersed fruits.

Figure 12.10 Wind-dispersed fruits.

The flesh of succulent fruits often has a bright colour and is eaten by many different mammals and birds. If the seeds are small they are eaten with the flesh of the fruit. The seed coats are resistant to the digestive processes of the animal and the seeds leave the animal's body in the faeces. The large seed in the stone of a succulent fruit may also be dispersed by animals. It is not eaten but is thrown away when the animal finishes its meal.

Many seeds which have a small mass, such as the willow herb, develop long hairs. The hairs increase the air resistance of the seed and allow it to be blown away. The dandelion has a fruit that forms a tuft of hairs. It acts as a parachute and slows down the fruit's sinking speed as the wind blows it along.

Seeds with a larger mass that use air to disperse them have parts of their fruit shaped into a wing. The South American tipu and the sycamore have winged fruits. The large surface area of the wing catches the wind as the fruit falls from the branches and allows it to be carried away from the tree on the air currents.

7 Summarise the text in a table to show how fruits and seeds are dispersed. Use the following terms: wind dispersal, animal dispersal, succulent fruits, hooked fruits, hard fruits, parachute fruits, winged fruits and explosive fruits. Give examples of each.

8 Why is a device that 'slows down the sinking speed' useful to wind-dispersed fruit?

9 Which kind of dispersal by animals provides the seeds with mineral salts? Explain your answer.

Figure 12.11   The South American tipu and its winged fruit.

Some plants, such as the lupin and the gorse, produce pods which dry and twist. The tension in the twisting pod becomes so great that the pod splits open and shoots the seeds out.

◆ SUMMARY ◆

♦ The life cycle of a plant begins with the seed (*see page 161*).
♦ The male part of the flower is the stamen. The anther on the stamen produces pollen (*see page 162*).
♦ The ovary is part of the female part of the flower. It contains ovules (*see page 162*).
♦ Pollination is the transfer of pollen from the anther to the stigma (*see page 162*).
♦ Wind and insect pollination are the two main kinds of pollination (*see page 163*).
♦ Fertilisation is the fusion of the male gamete nucleus with the female gamete nucleus to form a zygote (*see page 168*).
♦ The ovule develops into a seed after fertilisation (*see page 169*).
♦ The ovary develops into a fruit after fertilisation (*see page 169*).
♦ Seed dispersal reduces competition between seedlings (*see page 170*).
♦ There is a range of ways in which seeds and fruits are dispersed (*see pages 170–171*).

End of chapter question

1 Pollen grains will grow pollen tubes if they are placed in a sugar solution of a certain concentration. The results in the tables reflect results sometimes produced in investigations.

An experiment was set up to find out the concentration of sugar that would cause the pollen grains of a plant to produce pollen tubes. Here is a table of the results.

Table 12.1

Concentration of sugar solution/%	5	10	15	20
Number of pollen grains	20	20	20	20
Number of grains with tubes	4	18	3	0

a) What percentage of pollen grains produced tubes in each solution?
b) What would you expect the concentration of sugar in the stigmas of the flowers to be?

When the pollen of a second type of plant was investigated the following results were obtained.

Table 12.2

Concentration of sugar solution/%	5	10	15	20
Number of pollen grains	20	20	20	20
Number of grains with tubes	0	1	3	8

c) Why was it decided to take the investigation further?
d) What do you think was done to take the investigation further?

13

Food chains and food webs

The animal below is a killer whale. It is an organism at the end of a long food chain. The killer whale is trying to catch a seal. The seals, sensing that the killer whale is close by, have come out of the water. This is not stopping the killer whale from trying to catch one; it has swum quickly up the shore and tried to catch a seal by surprise in the surf.

In time, the seals will have to return to the sea to catch food for themselves. They feed on a variety of large fish which live off the shore. The large fish in turn feed on smaller fish; sometimes fish of their own species. The smaller fish feed on the larvae of crustaceans such as crabs and lobsters. These larvae do not remain on the rocky bed of the sea like their parents, but swim in the sunlit open waters of the sea. They form part of the plankton – a massive collection of tiny animals and algae. The crab larvae, along with all the other tiny animals, eat the algae. The algae do not eat anything. They are plant-like microbes belonging to the Protoctista kingdom. Like plants, algae make their own food through photosynthesis, and they use energy in sunlight to do it. It is the energy in sunlight that was trapped in algae and passed up the food chain that is being used in this picture by the killer whale as it tries to catch another meal.

1 Read the introductory text to this chapter again and construct a food chain from the information.

Figure 13.1 A killer whale.

Food chains around the world

There are food chains in every habitat in the world. Most are not as long as the one you have made in answer to Question 1. Food chains have a particular structure. They begin with an energy source, which is usually the Sun (see page 87). The first organism in the food chain is the one that extracts energy from sunlight and uses it to produce food. These organisms are called producers. Any green plant such as a moss, fern, conifer or flowering plant is a producer. Algae are producers too.

An organism that feeds on a producer is called a primary consumer. It in turn is eaten by a secondary consumer, which in turn is eaten by a tertiary consumer.

Figure 13.2 A female kangaroo with a joey in her pouch.

Figure 13.3 This frog is eating a damselfly.

We can use the structure of a food chain to compare food chains from around the world.

In the Australian outback, an area of desert and grassland, the main producer is grass. A primary consumer is a kangaroo and a secondary consumer is a wild dog (dingo).

In a tropical rainforest there are many different kinds of plants that are producers. For example a tree is a producer and the beetle that feeds on its leaves is a primary consumer. A tree frog feeds on the beetle and is therefore a secondary consumer. A tree snake feeds on the frog and is a tertiary consumer.

2 Construct three food chains from the information in this section.

3 How are producers in the food chains similar?

4 What features do you think secondary consumers have to help them catch their food?

For discussion

Some people think that the wolf should be re-introduced into countries where it is now extinct. Do you agree with this idea? Explain your answer.

In the mountains of Europe heather covers large areas of the ground. It is a producer. Mountain hares nibble its shoots and so are primary consumers. The golden eagle feeds on mountain hares and is a secondary consumer.

Figure 13.4 A golden eagle with its prey.

Decomposers

Figure 13.5 These Malaysian termites are feeding on leaf litter.

Not only do the living bodies of each species provide food for others but their dead bodies and waste are food too. The dead bodies of plants and animals are food for fungi, bacteria and small invertebrates that live in the soil and leaf litter. These organisms are called decomposers. When they have finished feeding, the bodies of plants and animals become reduced to the substances from which they were made. For example, the carbohydrates in a plant are broken down to carbon dioxide and water as the decomposers respire. Other substances are released from the plant's body as minerals and return to the soil. Decomposers are recyclers. They recycle the substances from which living things are made so that they can be used again.

5 Why are decomposers important? How do they affect you?

Pests

Pests are living organisms that damage the crops we grow for food. In the garden leaves can be eaten by slugs and snails. This reduces the plants' ability to make food and so a smaller crop is produced. If the damage is great, no crop will be produced. Beetle larvae in the soil can nibble the roots. This reduces the plants' ability to take up soil and water, so although the leaves are left intact their supply of some raw materials is reduced and less food is made.

On the farm insect pests can cause huge amounts of damage. Perhaps the worst insect pest of all is the locust. A swarm of locusts can eat entire fields of plants.

Even when a crop is harvested, it may be attacked where it is stored by pests such as mice and rats.

In some parts of the world where animals are farmed, secondary consumers can be a problem. In Europe, foxes can attack chickens and ducks. In Africa, lions can attack cattle.

Figure 13.6 This Filipino farmer is trying to protect his crop by pushing back a swarm of locusts.

The treatment of insect pests with chemicals is discussed in Chapter 15.

Biological pest control

Biological pest control is the use of one animal species to control the numbers of a pest. In 300 AD the Chinese began using biological pest control to protect their crops of mandarin oranges. These fruits are attacked by many insects, but it was discovered that a certain kind of large ant did not eat the crop but fed on the harmful insects. The ants were collected by filling sheep bladders with fat and putting them next to ants' nests. When the bladders were teeming with ants they were collected and placed in the orange trees. Bamboo poles were placed from one tree to the next in the orange grove so that the ants could move freely over all the trees. This form of biological control is still used today.

The biological control of other pests did not begin in other parts of the world until much more recent times. In Australia, the prickly pear was introduced as an ornamental garden plant but it soon started growing wild and became a weed. A moth which has a larva that feeds on the prickly pear was released among prickly pears, and in time their numbers were greatly reduced.

For discussion

Should only natural predators or primary consumers be used for biological control or should new kinds of animal be bred to control pests? Explain your answer.

6 Write a food chain for each item in the meal in Figure 13.7.
7 Write down the items in your breakfast. Make a food chain from each of these items. How many food chains feature animals as well as plants?
8 When do you feed as
  a) a primary consumer
  b) a secondary consumer?

Where are you in your food chains?

Where do all these foods come from? The cereal flakes are made from grains of maize – the grains you also eat as corn on the cob. The milk comes from a cow, and the cow gets its materials and energy to make milk from grass. The slice of bread is made from the flour of another cereal called wheat. It is spread with a margarine made from sunflower oil, and honey that is made from the nectar of flowers by bees.

Figure 13.7 Examples of some breakfast foods.

The energy in food chains

Figure 13.8 A bunch of radishes.

When you eat a radish you eat most of the plant except the leaves. If you were to eat a whole plant, you would not take in all the energy that the plant had trapped to make food. While the plant was growing it used some of the energy to stay alive and to build new materials so that its cells could grow and divide. In a similar way, if you were to be eaten by a predator it would not receive all the energy that you had taken in from your food. You use energy for life processes such as breathing, digesting your food and moving your body. You even lose some energy as heat to your surroundings. (In fact all living things lose some heat to their surroundings owing to the chemical reactions that take place inside them to keep them alive.) This means that as energy passes along a food chain some energy is lost from the food chain at every link.

Food webs

When several food chains are studied in a habitat some species may appear in it more than once. For example, a panda eats bamboo shoots and also eats fish. The two food chains it appears in are:

bamboo → panda

water plants → snails → fish → panda

This is then linked to make a food web.

Figure 13.9

A food web shows the movement of food through a habitat. It can also be used to help predict what might happen if one of the links in a food web was absent.

Look at Figure 13.10 and think of each animal shown there not just as one animal but as the whole population of that species of animal in the wood. If you think of each animal in the plural, such as voles and finches, it may help you think about animal populations.

Now imagine that the trees had a disease that made their leaves fall off. The caterpillars would starve and die, and they would not be available as food for the robins. This means that the robins must eat more beetles and woodlice if they are not to go hungry. The reduction in the number of woodlice would affect the shrews, as this is their only food. The beetle population would also fall, forcing the fox to search out more voles to eat.

9 How may the numbers of other species in the wood change if each of the following was removed in turn:
a) fox
b) seeds?

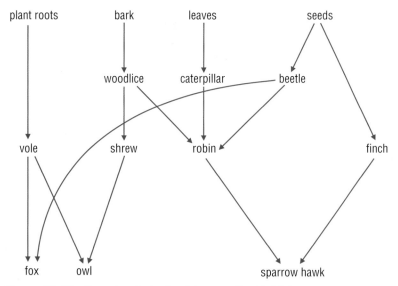

Figure 13.10   Examples of a food web in a woodland habitat.

Ecological pyramids

When a survey of a habitat is complete, ecologists can examine the relationships between the different species. They may find for example that deer depend on ferns for shelter in a wood, and that some birds use moss to line their nests. The major relationship between organisms in a habitat is the relationship through feeding. It is this relationship which interests ecologists (scientists who study ecosystems).

By studying the diets of animals in a habitat, ecologists can work out food chains and ecological pyramids.

Pyramid of numbers

The simplest type of ecological pyramid is the pyramid of numbers. The number of each species in the food chain in a habitat is estimated. The number of plants may be estimated using a quadrat (see page 72). The number of small animals may be estimated by using traps, nets and beating branches (see pages 74–76). The number of larger animals, such as birds, may be found by observing and counting.

An ecological pyramid is divided into tiers. There is one tier for each species in the food chain. The bottom tier is used to display information about the plant species or producer. The second tier is used for the primary consumer and the tiers above are used for other consumers in the food chain. The size of the tier represents the number of each species in the habitat. If the food chain:

$$\text{grass} \rightarrow \text{rabbit} \rightarrow \text{fox}$$

is represented as a pyramid of numbers, it will take the form shown in Figure 13.11.

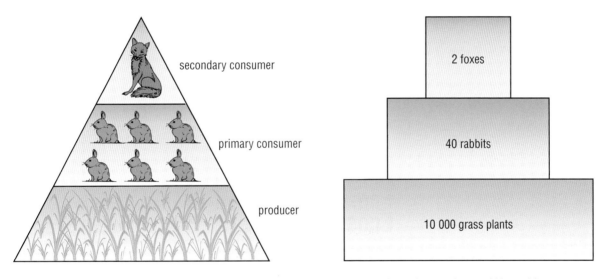

Figure 13.11 Food pyramid of numbers of grass plants, rabbits and foxes.

10 What would happen to the number of rabbits and grass plants if the number of foxes
   a) increased and
   b) decreased?

11 What would happen to the number of grass plants and foxes if the number of rabbits
   a) increased and
   b) decreased?

12 Why do the two food chains considered here produce different pyramids of numbers?

13 Why do you think there are usually more organisms at the bottom of a food chain?

Not all pyramids of numbers are widest at the base. For example, a tree creeper is a small brown bird with a narrow beak that feeds on insects that in turn feed on an oak tree. The food chain of this feeding relationship is:

oak tree → insects → tree creeper

When the food chain is studied further and a pyramid of numbers is displayed it appears as shown in Figure 13.12.

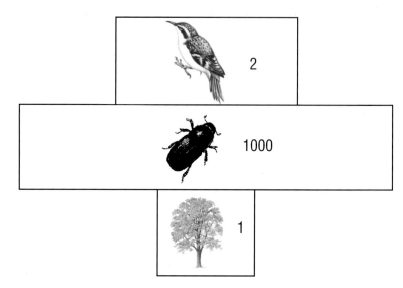

Figure 13.12 Pyramid of numbers of oak tree, insects and tree creepers.

14 Living things need water in their bodies to survive. What happens to the living things used to work out a pyramid of biomass? Explain your answer.

15 If you drew a pyramid of biomass for the food chain

   oak tree → insects → tree
   creeper

   what do you think it would look like? How would it compare with the pyramid of numbers? Explain any differences that you would see.

16 How might studying ecosystems help to conserve endangered species?

Pyramid of biomass

The amount of matter in a body is found by drying it to remove all water then weighing it. This amount of matter is called the biomass. Ecologists find measuring biomass useful as it tells them how much matter is locked up in each species of a food chain.

Ecosystems

Decomposers form one of the links between the living things in a community and the non-living environment. Green plants form the second link. When a community of living things, such as those that make up a wood, interact with the non-living environment – the decomposers releasing minerals, carbon dioxide and water into the environment and then plants taking them in again – the living and non-living parts form an ecological system or ecosystem. An ecosystem can be quite small, such as a pond, or as large as a lake or a forest.

Working out how everything interacts is very complicated but is essential to ecologists if they are to understand how each species in the ecosystem survives and how it affects other species and the non-living part of the ecosystem. Figure 13.13 shows how the living and non-living parts of a very simple ecosystem react together.

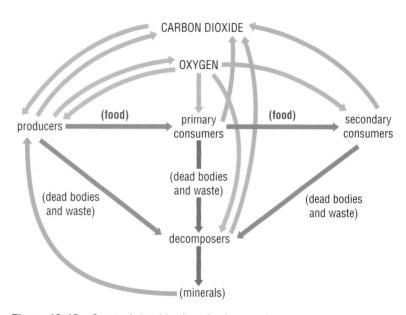

Figure 13.13   Some relationships in a simple ecosystem.

17 An aquarium tank set up with pond life is an ecosystem. See Figure 13.14.

  a) Which are the producers and which are the consumers?

  b) Construct some food chains that might occur in the tank.

  c) Where are the decomposers?

  d) Give examples of the ways the living things react to their non-living environment.

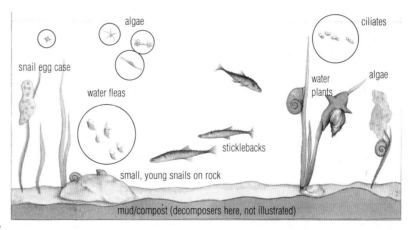

Figure 13.14   An aquarium with pond life. The circled organisms are greatly magnified.

How populations change

If an area of ground is cleared of vegetation it will soon be colonised by new plants and animals. The following is an account of how an area of soil could be colonised. The colonisation is much simpler than occurs naturally so that the ways the plants and animals interact can be seen more clearly.

A seed lands in the centre of a soil patch and germinates. The plant is an ephemeral (has a very short life cycle) and is soon fully grown and producing flowers and seeds. The seeds are scattered over the whole area. They all germinate and grow so the population of the ephemeral plants increases.

There are perennial plants (which flower and continue to grow for several years) outside the area of cleared soil that have stems with broad leaves that cover the ground. As the population of the ephemeral plants increases, the perennial plants grow into the area of cleared soil. The two kinds of plants compete for light, water and minerals in the soil. As the numbers of both plants increase, the competition between them also increases. The perennials compete more successfully than the ephemeral plants for the resources in the habitat and produce more offspring. The broad leaves of the perennial plants cover the soil and prevent seeds from landing there and germinating. The leaves may also grow over the young ephemeral seedlings. In time the ephemeral plants that are producing seeds will die and the stems and broad leaves of the perennials could cover them too.

Herbivorous insects land on some of the perennial plants and start to feed on their leaves. They feed and breed and as their numbers increase they spread out over other perennial plants in the area. The population of the perennial plants in the area begins to fall and the population of ephemerals, which are not eaten by the insects, begins to rise.

A few carnivorous insects land in the centre of the patch. They clamber about on the plants and feed on the herbivorous insects. The well-fed carnivorous insects breed and their population increases. The population of the herbivorous insects starts to fall.

18 In what ways do the two kinds of plants compete for the resources?

19 If the herbivorous insects had not arrived what do you think would have happened to the two populations of plants?

20 How did the arrival of the herbivorous insects affect your prediction in Question 19? Explain your answer.

21 What effect do the carnivorous insects have on the population of
a) herbivorous insects and
b) ephemeral plants?

22 How may the population of herbivorous insects change over a period of time?

23 Draw a freehand graph to show the change in size of the population of
  a) herbivorous insects and
  b) carnivorous insects over time.

24 a) How does the population of snowshoe hares vary over the 90 years?
  b) How does the population of lynx vary over the 90 years?
  c) Do the populations vary in exactly the same way or does one population lag behind the other?
  d) It has been suggested that the way the population varies is due to the way the lynx preys on the snowshoe hare. Do you think this is an accurate suggestion? Explain your answer.

How populations change with time

A population of a species is the number of individuals present in a habitat. The survival of a species in a habitat depends upon many factors (see Chapter 5). As prey animals are affected by predators and predators depend on prey, it may seem reasonable to suspect that their population sizes might be linked.

Charles Elton (1900–1991) was an English ecologist who studied some unusual data to investigate the relationship between prey and predator. He used the records of the Hudson Bay Company in Canada for the years 1860–1935. The Hudson Bay Company traded in animal pelts and the records showed the number of pelts supplied to the company by trappers. Elton studied the numbers of snowshoe hare and lynx pelts supplied by the trappers. The number of pelts of each species supplied in each year indicated the size of the species population in that year. Figure 13.15 shows the graphs produced from the data.

Predicting changes in populations

The changing size of the human population can be predicted by comparing birth rates with death rates. The birth rate is the number of babies born per 1000 people in the population in a year. The death rate is the number of people dying per 1000 people in the population in a year.

If the birth rate is greater than the death rate the population will increase in size. If the death rate is greater than the birth rate the population will decrease in size. If the birth rate and the death rate are the same the population will remain unchanged.

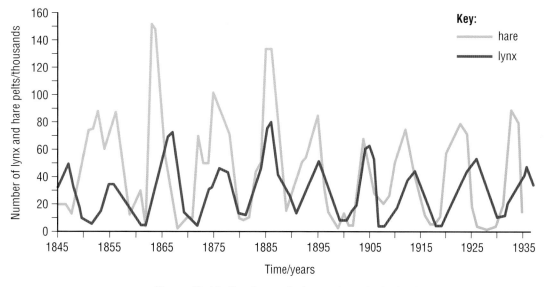

Figure 13.15 The changes in the numbers of animal pelts supplied by trappers to the Hudson Bay Company.

Birth rates, death rates and conservation

Many endangered mammal species have been reduced to a small world population by hunting. The animals have been killed more quickly than they can reproduce. If the death rate exceeds the birth rate the mammal species is set on a course for extinction. Many mammals are now threatened with this course.

They can be helped by raising their birth rate and reducing their death rate. Zoos can help increase the size of the world population of some endangered animal species. They do this by increasing the birth rate by making all the adult animals in their care healthy enough to breed and by providing extra care in the rearing of the young. Zoos also reduce the death rate by protecting the animals from predation. In many countries reserves have been set up in which endangered animals live naturally but are protected from hunting by humans. This reduces the death rate, which in turn increases the birth rate as more animals survive to reach maturity and breed.

Figure 13.16 A Java rhinoceros which is threatened with extinction.

For discussion

Large mammals need large areas of natural habitat to support a large population. With the increasing human population why is it difficult to conserve these large areas? Explain your answer.

The human population

The human population of the Earth reached 1 billion (a thousand million) in 1804. Two hundred years later the figure was over six times greater. Table 13.1 shows the rise in population to 6 billion, and the estimated population in the future.

25 If the estimates are correct how old will you be when the world population reaches
  a) 7 billion,
  b) 8 billion,
  c) 9 billion?

26 Plot a graph of the data in the table. What might the population be in 2100?

Table 13.1

Date	Population (billion)
1804	1
1927	2
1960	3
1974	4
1987	5
1999	6
2013	7
2028	8
2054	9
2183	10

For discussion

Why do you think the human population has grown so large?

◆ SUMMARY ◆

◆ Food chains begin with an energy source (*see page 174*).

◆ The first organism in a food chain is called a producer (*see page 174*).

◆ A producer is eaten by a primary consumer (*see page 174*).

◆ A primary consumer is eaten by a secondary consumer (*see page 174*).

◆ Decomposers break down dead bodies and wastes of living things into simple substances (*see page 175*).

◆ Pests are living organisms that can damage crops (*see page 176*).

◆ Some energy is lost from the food chain as it passes along the chain (*see page 178*).

◆ Food chains link together to form food webs (*see page 179*).

◆ A pyramid of numbers shows the numbers of each species at each link in the food chain (*see page 181*).

◆ The living and non-living parts of a habitat form an ecosystem (*see page 182*).

◆ Populations of a species in a habitat change (*see page 184*).

◆ Birth rates and death rates are important in predicting changes in populations (*see page 185*).

End of chapter questions

You may wish to read about herbivores, carnivores and omnivores on pages 77–79 before you answer this question.

1 Construct a food web for the African plains from the following information.

Giraffes feed on trees, elephants feed on trees, eland feed on trees and bushes, hunting dogs feed on eland and zebra, finches feed on bushes, mice feed on roots, baboons feed on roots and locusts, gazelles, zebras and locusts feed on grass, foxes feed on mice, lions feed on eland, zebra and gazelle, hawks feed on finches, eagles feed on baboons, foxes and gazelles.

(continued)

You may like to write the name of each living thing on a separate card and arrange the cards on a sheet of paper. You could write arrows on the paper between the cards but use pencil at first as you may find that you have to move the cards about to make the food web tidy.

2 Use the food web you have made for Question 1 to answer these questions.
   a) Which living organisms are producers?
   b) Which animals are herbivores?
   c) Which animals are carnivores?
   d) Which animal is an omnivore?

3 An investigation on the populations of two microbes was carried out. One microbe called paramecium (a ciliate) was the predator and the other, yeast (see page 50), was the prey. The microbes were kept in a sugar solution in a glass container. The sugar provided food for the yeast. Figure 13.7 shows how the populations varied over a period of 19 days.

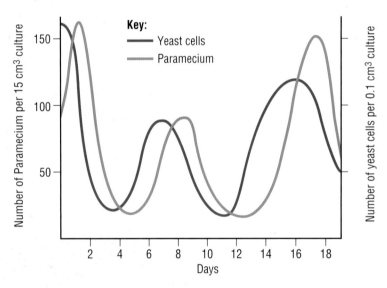

Figure 13.17

   a) When the population of yeast rose from its lowest to its highest, what happened to the population of paramecium?
   b) Suggest a reason for your answer to part **a)**.
   c) When the population of yeast fell from its highest to its lowest, what happened to the population of paramecium?
   d) Suggest a reason for your answer to part **c)**.
   e) Do you think the results of this experiment provide more reliable evidence for the relationship between prey and predator than the data provided by the Hudson Bay Company (see page 185)? Explain your answer.

14

Adaptation and selection

Every living thing has a certain basic body plan. For example, a flowering plant has a root, a stem, leaves and flowers, and a bird has a head with a beak and a body with two wings and two legs and a tail. However, every living thing also has special features which help it live in its surroundings. These features are called adaptations. For example, a flowering plant which grows in a windy habitat has a short stem so that there is less chance of it being blown over. The short stem is an adaptation to the habitat. A heron is a bird with very long legs and a pointed spear-shaped beak. These two features are adaptations to the heron's basic body plan. They help the heron survive by allowing it to wade into deep water and spear fish with its beak.

Figure 14.1   A heron fishing in a river.

Adaptations to the seasons

There are only a few habitats, such as caves, where the environmental conditions remain the same throughout the year. In most habitats there are periods in the year called seasons during which the weather has a particular feature. A habitat might have a dry season and a wet season, or the cold weather of winter and the warm weather of summer.

1 Why is it an advantage for a woodland plant to grow before the trees come into leaf?

2 Why don't insects such as butterflies spend the winter in their active stages of caterpillar and adult?

3 Why is it an advantage for birds and other animals to rear as many young as they can in summer?

Seasons in a European woodland

In Europe there are four seasons of the year – winter, spring, summer and autumn.

Deciduous trees adapt to the cold icy weather of winter by losing their leaves. Deciduous trees are trees with large flat broad leaves. These leaves lose a great deal of water. In winter, the ground is often frozen so the water cannot pass into the roots. If the trees kept their leaves, they would lose water but would not be able to replace it. They would dry out and die.

Most insects spend winter in a stage of their life where they do not need to move or search for food. These stages are the egg and pupa stage. Animals such as hedgehogs and bats, which feed on insects, hibernate.

In spring as the ground warms up, woodland plants such as snowdrops and bluebells grow from bulbs and produce leaves and flowers. These plants use the sunlight shining through the bare branches to make food, and early hatching insects to pollinate them. As spring goes on the deciduous trees put out their leaves and flowers. Hibernating animals wake up and search for food. Woodland birds build nests and begin to rear young. In summer the leaves of the trees form a shady canopy over the woodland floor. Few plants are in flower there now. The birds may lay second or even third clutches of eggs and raise more young. Caterpillars feed on the leaves.

Figure 14.2 A European woodland in spring.

In the autumn the weather becomes cooler again. Trees produce fruits such as nuts and berries, which are eaten by many mammals and birds. The leaves of the deciduous trees lose their chlorophyll. At this time brown and yellow pigments in the leaves give them their colour. The trees release waste products into their leaves, and in time the leaves fall. Animals that hibernate gorge themselves on food to build up fat. This is the energy store which they will use through the winter months in order to stay alive.

4 State two ways in which losing leaves in autumn helps deciduous trees.

Seasons on an African grassland

In the Serengeti National Park in East Africa there is a wet and a dry season. The plains are covered by long grass which is eaten by huge numbers of herbivores. Zebras eat the tough tops to the grass stalks, which contain the wind-pollinated flowers. Wildebeest (gnu) feed on the more succulent leaves lower down the plant, while the young shoots and the seeds on the ground are eaten by gazelles.

During the wet season the animals migrate to a drier part of the plains in the south. At the beginning of the dry season they move to the west where there is a little rainfall and the grass is still thick. In the middle of the dry season they move to a region where the soil is particularly fertile and the plants are still edible.

5 What are the advantages of a large group of animals moving round together in their habitat?

6 A zebra has a height at the shoulder of 1.2–1.4 metres. A wildebeest has a shoulder height of 1.0–1.3 metres. A gazelle has a shoulder height of 51–89 centimetres. Use this information and the information in the text to describe and explain the order in which the animals would move through an area of long grass.

7 Do you think carnivores such as lions migrate too? Explain your answer.

Figure 14.3 A herd of zebras on the move.

Adaptations to a habitat

Each habitat has a set of environmental conditions. If an organism is to survive there it must adapt to them.

Plants

Mangrove swamp

Mangrove swamps occur along the coasts of many countries in tropical climates. The mud in which plants grow is moved by the rising and falling of the tides.

Mangrove trees have adapted to the tides by growing many roots from their trunks. The roots spread out over a wide area and dip down into the mud to hold the tree in place. Mangrove trees also have seeds that are adapted for survival in this habitat of moving mud. When the fruit forms it remains attached to the tree. The seed germinates using moisture in the humid air, and the seedling grows to about 25 centimetres before it leaves the tree. As the seedling falls it remains vertical so that when it hits the mud the root forces its way in and holds the plant in place.

8 What do you think would happen to the trees if they did not have the extra roots?

9 Why is it beneficial for the seeds to germinate and seedlings to grow while still on the tree?

Figure 14.4 A mangrove swamp. The roots are visible because it is low tide.

Tropical rainforest

The main feature of a tropical rainforest is its thick forest canopy of branches and leaves. This shades the ground below. When seeds fall to the ground and germinate the seedlings that are produced struggle to find enough light to survive, and as a result many die. The seeds of the strangler fig are capable of growing in the compost that develops in the forks of tree branches. This means that as the seed is nearer the canopy it has a greater chance of receiving enough light to survive.

At first the seedling uses water in the compost in the fork but as it grows it needs more. The plant responds to this by growing a root down the side of the tree to find the soil on the ground. Once the root has reached the ground it can take up more water and nutrients and the rest of the plant can start to grow upwards into the canopy. The plant continues to send down more roots, and in time they form a basket-like support around the tree. The water and minerals provided by the extra roots allow the plant to grow so large that its leaves overshadow the tree on which it is growing.

In time the roots develop such a rigid hold on the tree trunk that the xylem and phloem tissues (see page 137), which transport food and water inside the tree, are crushed and the tree dies. The strangler fig continues to thrive and takes over the space originally occupied by the tree.

10 What do you think might happen to strangler fig seeds that fell into forks in the tree high in the canopy which had very little compost?

11 How did the leafy shoot of the strangler fig affect the tree it was growing around?

Figure 14.5   A strangler fig around a tree.

Keystone species

A keystone species in a habitat is one that helps the survival of a large number of other species.

The strangler fig is an example of a keystone species. Its fruit provides food for hornbills, monkeys, parrots, pigeons and many insects. The fruit is often produced at times when other plants are not producing fruit, so it helps to provide a constant food supply to many rainforest herbivores. If the strangler fig was removed from the forest a great many other species would suffer, and possibly become extinct.

When trees are removed from a rainforest for timber, care must be taken to consider plants like the strangler fig and preserve them. This can be particularly difficult where the strangler figs attack the trees that loggers want to cut down and sell.

For discussion

Can you work out a strategy for maintaining strangler figs in a forest while still extracting some timber by controlled logging?

Animals

Adaptations to a fast flowing river

The tiny remains of plants and animals are washed down streams and rivers and form a food supply for any animals that are adapted to live there. The major problem for animals in such a habitat is the current, which will carry them away. Many invertebrates have solved this problem by developing ways of holding onto the river bed and presenting as small a surface as possible to the water rushing by them.

Stonefly and mayfly nymphs have legs adapted for gripping rocks. Their bodies are flat and held close to the rocks so the water flows over them. Leeches have suckers to hold onto rocks. The river limpet has a foot which acts as a sucker, and it also has a streamlined shell (see Keys page 53) to help the water flow smoothly over it.

12 Where do you think the tiny remains of plants and animals in the stream come from?

13 Why should animals adapt to live in fast flowing water when there are regions of slow moving water in a river?

Adaptations to tree tops

The rainforest canopy is the habitat of many species of monkey. The monkey's body has many adaptations to tree top life. Monkeys have small, lightweight bodies that allow them to climb out on to slender branches to collect food. Monkeys have an opposable thumb and big toe which allow them to grip the branches firmly.

A monkey will often jump from one branch to another or even from tree to tree. When it does this it needs to be able to judge distance. Both eyes face forwards so that their fields of vision overlap. This allows monkeys to judge distances accurately so that they can land safely.

Figure 14.6 Monkey in the canopy in a tropical rainforest.

14 How would the feeding activities of a monkey be affected if it had a large heavy body?

15 Although monkeys have good eyesight they also have good hearing and communicate a great deal by sound in the forest canopy. Why is this?

Monkeys have tails which are used to help them keep their balance as they run and jump about. In South America monkeys such as the spider monkey have a prehensile tail. This acts as a fifth limb, and they use it to grip onto or even hang from branches as they feed.

Adaptations for survival

Organisms have a range of adaptations to their habitat but some play a key part in their survival.

Plants

Pebble plant

Pebble plants grow in the deserts of Southern Africa. Unlike cacti they protect themselves from browsing animals by camouflaging themselves to look like stones. A pebble plant has only two leaves and these are small and close to the ground so they are difficult for browsers to reach. The two leaves make an almost spherical shape. This shape allows the plant to have a large volume for storing water, yet presents only the smallest possible surface area to the heat of the Sun's rays.

16 What might happen to a pebble plant in the heat of the Sun if it had a large flat surface with a thin body like a pancake?

Figure 14.7 Pebble plants in a desert.

17 Why must the tumbleweed shoot die to spread the seeds?

18 What adaptations would a tumbleweed need so that the shoot does not have to die to spread the seeds but can plant itself again?

Tumbleweed

Plants which grow tall can disperse their seeds into the wind. The seeds may be blown a long distance before they reach the ground. Woody plants on some grasslands cannot grow tall because the winds would blow them over, so they must disperse their seeds in another way. The tumbleweed solves this problem by breaking off its shoot full of seeds – the dead shoot can then be blown over the grassland by the wind and lose its seeds as it goes.

Figure 14.8 The shoot system of a mature tumbleweed. It has snapped off above the root and curled into a ball. As it is blown by the wind it sheds its seeds.

Animals

Pit viper

The pit viper has two pits on its head which are about 4 mm wide and 6 mm deep. They are packed with receptors which are sensitive to heat. The receptors are so sensitive that they can detect changes of 0.002 °C. This means that an object 0.1 °C warmer or cooler than the surroundings can be detected by the snake. These heat-sensitive organs help the pit viper to find food, such as mammals and birds, in dark places.

Figure 14.9 A pit viper.

19 Pit vipers hunt through the grass in the daytime looking for passages which mice have recently used. How could the pit viper tell by using its pits if a mouse had travelled along very recently?

Mammals and birds are described as warm-blooded. This is misleading because on a hot day animals such as reptiles can be warmer. Mammals and birds regulate their body temperature so that it stays constant, and usually above that of its surroundings. This makes birds and mammals suitable prey for pit vipers. The pit viper has a pit on each side of its face just in front of its eyes. This means that the areas detected by the pits overlap just like the fields of vision in monkeys (see page 194), and helps the snake to judge distances, so that it knows when to strike with its fangs and poison.

Flying fish

Flying fish are found in tropical seas. They feed on the plankton close to the surface, where they are the prey of the dolphin fish. The dolphin fish behaves in some ways like a dolphin, such as jumping out of the water. When a dolphin fish starts an attack, the flying fish swims faster and faster. It moves upwards in the water, and when it is travelling at about 60 kph it breaks through the sea's surface and glides through the air on its long wide front fins. The lower part of the tail fin is

Figure 14.10 Flying fish.

20 Do you think that the flying fish is free from predators once it has left the water? Explain your answer.

also long, and as the fish rises into the air it waves its tail fin 50 times a second so the lower fin repeatedly pushes against the water and gives the fish extra thrust to make its flight. Once out of the water the flying fish can travel up to 200 metres in the air and escape from the dolphin fish.

Inherited characteristics

In Chapter 4 we looked at how living things vary within a species. Now we will consider how living things vary within a species from one generation to the next. If you look at two generations of a species you will see that both generations have some identical features, and that some features may vary from one generation to the next.

In the dalmatian dog, for example, the parents and offspring each have a head, four legs, a tail and a spotty body. These features are identical. However, the puppies have different spot patterns from their parents and from each other. They may also have longer or shorter tails than their parents, and longer or shorter ears.

The features that a body possesses are also known as its characteristics. Information about the characteristics is passed from one generation to the next in the reproductive cells. In plants, for example, the information is passed from the parent plants to the seeds by the male cell in the pollen and the female cell in the ovule (see page 168).

Figure 14.11 Dalmatian mother with litter of well grown pups.

The cells carry information about the characteristics in their nuclei. Each nucleus has threads in it called chromosomes.

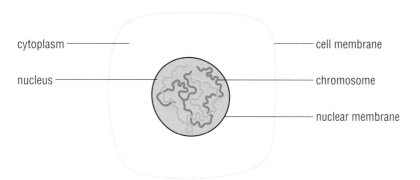

cytoplasm ——————— ——————— cell membrane

nucleus ——————— ——————— chromosome

——————— nuclear membrane

Figure 14.12 Chromosomes in the nucleus of a cell.

On the chromosomes are regions called genes. Each gene is made from DNA, and carries information about characteristics such as the colour of the petals or the colour of the eyes. The offspring receive genes from both parents and these join together in such a way that makes sure that the offspring have the major features of the species, such as a head, four legs and tail in dogs, but also have some features which vary slightly, such as tail and ear length.

Mendelian genetics

Gregor Mendel (1822–1884) was an Austrian monk who studied mathematics and natural history. He set up experiments to investigate how features in one generation of pea plants were passed on to the next. Pea flowers self-pollinate. When Mendel wished to control the way the flowers pollinated he cut off the anthers of one flower, collected pollen from another flower and brushed it on to the stigma of the first. He completed his task by tying a muslin bag around the first flower to prevent any other pollen from reaching it.

Mendel performed thousands of experiments and used his mathematical knowledge to set out his results and to look for patterns in the way that the plant features were inherited. He suggested that each feature was controlled by an inherited factor. He also suggested that each factor had two sets of instructions and that parents pass on one set of instructions each to their offspring. Many years later it was discovered that Mendel's 'factors' were genes.

Mendel's work was published by a natural history society but its importance was not realised until 16 years after his death. At that time Hugo de Vries (1848–1935), a Dutch botanist, had been studying how plants pass on their characteristics from generation to generation. He was checking through published reports of experiments when he discovered Mendel's work. De Vries's work supported Mendel's but he also made another discovery. He had studied the evening primrose, a plant that had been newly introduced into Holland, and found that the plants occasionally produced a new variety that was quite different from the others. This new variety was caused by mutation. Although mutations had been seen in herds of livestock before, where the odd animal was sometimes called a 'sport', de Vries was the first to introduce the idea of mutations into scientific studies.

Figure A Short-legged sheep mutation.

1 Why did Mendel cut out the anthers of some flowers?
2 Why did Mendel tie a muslin bag around the flower in the experiment?
3 What is the value of performing a large number of experiments?
4 Could money be saved on fencing if you farmed short-legged sheep? Explain your answer.
5 Mutation means change. Why is it a good word to describe a new variety of a species?

DNA

Genes are made from a substance called deoxyribonucleic acid which is usually shortened to DNA. The first work on investigating the chemicals in cell nuclei was carried out in 1869 by Johann Friedrich Miescher (1844–1895). He used the white cells in pus and the substance he discovered was called nuclein. Over the next 84 years generations of scientists made investigations on this substance. Rosalind Franklin (1920–1958) studied the structure of molecules by firing X-rays at them. In 1951 she investigated DNA in this way and her results suggested to her that it could be made of two coiled strands, but she was not sure. In 1953 James Watson and Francis Crick, using some of Franklin's results to help them, worked out that DNA is made from long strands of chemicals that are coiled together to make a structure called a double helix. The chemicals are arranged in a sequence that acts as a code. The code provides the cell with instructions on how to make the other chemicals that it needs to stay alive and develop properly.

Barbara McClintock (1902–1992) was a geneticist who studied maize – the plant that provides sweetcorn. While she was still a student she worked out a way of relating the different chromosomes in the nucleus to the features of the plant. Later, in the 1940s, she discovered that the genes on a chromosome could change position. They became known as 'jumping genes'. This discovery did not fit in with the way genes were thought to act and her work was

(continued)

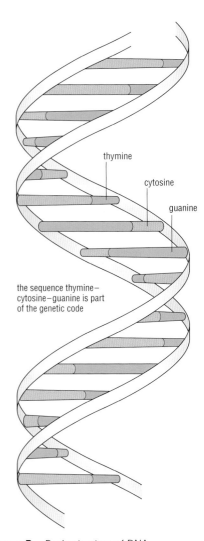

thymine

cytosine

guanine

the sequence thymine–
cytosine–guanine is part
of the genetic code

Figure B   Basic structure of DNA.

Figure C   Barbara McClintock.

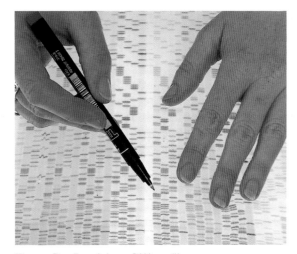

Figure D   Examining a DNA profile.

not accepted by other scientists. But in the 1970s, during investigations by scientists on the DNA molecule, it was found that parts of the DNA broke off and moved to other parts of the chromosome. McClintock's work was proved to be correct and in 1983 she received the Nobel Prize for Physiology or Medicine.

As each person's DNA is unique it can be used for identification purposes. A person's DNA profile (sometimes called a DNA fingerprint) can be made from cells in the saliva or the blood. The DNA is chopped up by enzymes and its pieces are separated into a gel in a process like chromatography. (Remember that chromatography is the process used to separate colours in an ink by putting a drop of ink onto a paper and allowing water to soak through it.) The pattern of the pieces looks like a bar code on an item of goods. Closely related people have more similar profiles than those who are not related.

For discussion

How could DNA be used to investigate a crime?

How firmly should scientists hold their views?

21 In a key about fish the species are identified by the length of their bodies and by their body mass. Is this key reliable? Explain your answer.

Keys

Keys are used to help identify living things. You may wish to look back to page 52 and revise your work on keys. They are made by considering features in a species which do not vary. Features which might change due to growth, for example, are not used.

◆ SUMMARY ◆

- ◆ Living things in a habitat are adapted to the seasons (*see page 189*).
- ◆ Plants are adapted to the environmental conditions in their habitat (*see page 192*).
- ◆ Animals are adapted to the environmental conditions in their habitat (*see page 194*).
- ◆ Plants have adaptations which help them survive in their habitat (*see page 195*).
- ◆ Animals have adaptations which help them survive in their habitat (*see page 196*).
- ◆ Living things have characteristics which they inherit from the generation before them (*see page 198*).
- ◆ Keys use features of a species that do not vary to help in identification (*see page 202*).

End of chapter question

1 This is a fictional habitat for which you must design an animal with adaptations to take advantage of the changing food supply.

In the habitat is a large lake, rich in small invertebrates. Around the edge are tall trees which produce leaves only in the top branches. Once a year the lake dries up, and at this time caterpillars hatch to feed on the leaves. After a few weeks they change to flying insects. The flying insects spend most of the next few weeks either in the air or resting on the branches. They die when the rains return and the lake fills up again.

You may like to start by thinking about an animal swimming in the lake. It can be large or small and have changes in its life cycle, like a frog.

15

Human influence on the environment

Humans in the environment

The first people used natural materials such as stone, wood, animal skins, bones, antlers and shells. They shaped materials using flint knives and axes. When they discovered fire they also discovered the changes that heat could make.

First they saw how it changed food, and later it is believed that they saw how metal was produced from hot rocks around a camp fire. In time, they learned how to extract metals from rocks by smelting and to use the metals to make a range of products (see Figure 15.1).

Figure 15.1 A Bronze Age village scene.

The human population was only small when metal smelting was discovered, and the smoke and smell from this process caused little pollution. As the human population grew, the demand for metal and other products such as pottery and glass increased. All the processing in the manufacture of these products had to be done by hand. Although there would be some pollution around the places where people gathered to make these products, the world environment was not threatened.

About 200 years ago it was discovered how machines could be used in manufacturing processes, and the Industrial Revolution began. Machines could be used to produce more products than would be produced by people working on their own.

This meant that large amounts of fuel were needed to work the machines and air pollution increased (see Figure 15.2). Larger amounts of raw materials were needed and more habitats were destroyed in order to obtain them. More waste products were produced, increasing water and land pollution as the industrial manufacturing processes developed. The world population also increased, causing an increased demand for more materials which in turn led to more pollution and habitat destruction.

Figure 15.2   The smoky skyline of Glasgow in the mid-19th Century.

1 What were the first materials people used?

2 Why did the pollution caused by manufacturing materials not cause a serious threat to the environment until the Industrial Revolution?

3 Why did people belive it was safe to release wastes into the environment?

At first, and for many years, it was believed that the air could carry away the fumes and make them harmless, and that chemicals could be flushed into rivers and the sea where they would be diluted and become harmless. Also, the ways various chemical wastes could affect people were unknown.

An awareness of the dangers of pollution increased in the latter half of the 20th Century, and in many countries today steps are being taken to control it and develop more efficient ways of manufacturing materials.

For discussion

Some people belive that we must go back to the lifestyles of our earlier ancestors if the planet is to be saved. How realistic is this idea? Explain your answer.

The Earth's changing atmosphere

Studies from astronomy and geology have shown that the Solar System formed from a huge cloud of gas and dust in space. The Earth is one of the planets formed from this cloud. The surface of the Earth was punctured with erupting volcanoes for a billion years after it formed. The gases escaping from inside the Earth through the volcanoes formed an atmosphere composed of water vapour, carbon dioxide and nitrogen.

Figure A   A smoking volcano in Indonesia.

Three billion years ago the first plants developed. They produced oxygen as a waste product of photosynthesis. As the plants began to flourish in both sea and fresh water and on the land, the amount of oxygen in the atmosphere increased. It reacted with ammonia to produce nitrogen.

Figure B   Some early land plants were probably similar to modern-day ferns.

(continued)

Bacteria developed which survived by using energy from the breakdown of nitrates in the soil. In this process more nitrogen was produced. In time, nitrogen and oxygen became the two major gases of the atmosphere. Between 15 and 30 kilometres above the Earth, the ultraviolet rays of the Sun reacted with oxygen to produce ozone. An ozone molecule is formed from three oxygen atoms. It prevents ultraviolet radiation, which is harmful to life, reaching the Earth's surface. If the ozone layer had not developed, life might not have evolved to cover such large areas of the planet's surface as it does today.

Owing to the activities of humans, the atmosphere today contains increasing amounts of carbon dioxide, large amounts of sulphur dioxide and chlorofluorocarbons (CFCs) which have destroyed large portions of the ozone layer.

1 How has the composition of the atmosphere changed since the Earth first formed?

2 What has changed the composition of the atmosphere?

3 The atmospheres of Venus and Mars are like the atmosphere of the Earth in the first million years of its history. What can you infer from this information?

For discussion

How is the change in the ozone layer affecting people today?

For discussion

How would our lives change if power stations could no longer supply us with electricity?

Air pollution

Every day we burn large amounts of fuel such as coal and oil in power stations to produce electricity. This provides us with light, warmth and power. The power is used in all kinds of industries for the manufacture of a wide range of things, from clothes to cars. In the home, electricity runs washing machines, fridges and microwave ovens. It provides power for televisions, radios and computers. When coal and oil are burned, however, they produce carbon dioxide, carbon monoxide, sulphur dioxide, oxides of nitrogen and soot particles that make smoke.

Figure 15.3 Electricity makes our lives more comfortable.

Carbon dioxide

Carbon dioxide is described as a greenhouse gas because the carbon dioxide in the atmosphere acts like the glass in a greenhouse. It allows heat energy from the Sun to pass through it to the Earth, but prevents much of the heat energy radiating from the Earth's surface from passing out into space. The heat energy remains in the atmosphere and warms it up. The warmth of the Earth has allowed millions of different life forms to develop, and it keeps the planet habitable.

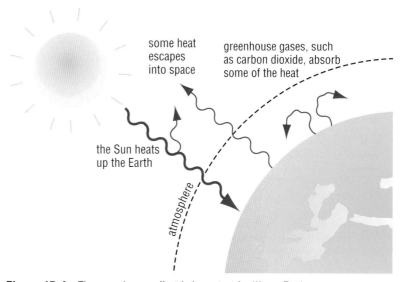

Figure 15.4 The greenhouse effect is important for life on Earth.

In the past the level of carbon dioxide in the atmosphere has remained low, but the level is now beginning to rise. The extra carbon dioxide will probably trap more heat energy in the atmosphere. A rise in the temperature of the atmosphere will cause an expansion of the water in the oceans. It will also cause the melting of the ice cap on the continent of Antarctica, and this water will then flow into the expanding ocean waters. Both of these events will lead to a raising of the sea level and a change in the climate for almost all parts of the Earth. The rise in temperature is known as global warming.

Carbon monoxide

Carbon monoxide is a very poisonous gas. It readily combines with the red pigment haemoglobin in the blood. Haemoglobin carries oxygen round the body but if carbon monoxide is inhaled, it combines with the haemoglobin and stops the oxygen being transported.

Acid rain makers

Sulphur dioxide is produced by the combustion of sulphur in a fuel when the fuel is burned. Sulphur dioxide reacts with water vapour and oxygen in the air to form sulphuric acid. This may fall to the ground as acid rain or snow.

Oxides of nitrogen are converted to nitric acid in the atmosphere and this also falls to the ground as acid rain or as snow.

Acid rain

When acid rain reaches the ground it drains into the soil, dissolves some of the minerals there and carries them away. This process is called leaching. Some of the minerals are needed for the healthy growth of plants. Without the minerals the plants become stunted and may die (see Figure 15.5).

Figure 15.5 Spruce trees in Bulgaria damaged by acid rain.

The acid rain drains into rivers and lakes and lowers the pH of the water. Many forms of water life are sensitive to the pH of the water and cannot survive if it is too acidic. If the pH changes, they die and the animals that feed on them, such as fish, may also die.

Acid rain leaches aluminium ions out of the soil. If they reach a high concentration in the water the gills of fish are affected. It causes the fish to suffocate.

Soot and smog

Figure 15.6 The London smog of 1952.

4 What property of soot particles affects photosynthesis?

5 Why is carbon monoxide a deadly gas?

6 A lake is situated near a factory that burns coal. How may the lake be affected in years to come if
   a) there is no smoke control at the factory,
   b) there is no smoke control worldwide?
Explain your answers.

The soot particles in the air from smoke settle on buildings and plant life. They make buildings dirty and form black coatings on their outer surfaces. When soot covers leaves, it cuts down the amount of light reaching the leaf cells and slows down photosynthesis.

As well as being used in industry, coal used to be the main fuel for heating homes in the United Kingdom until the 1950s. In foggy weather the smoke from the coal combined with water droplets in the fog to form smog. The water droplets absorbed the soot particles and chemicals in the smoke and made a very dense cloud at ground level, through which it was difficult to see.

When people inhaled air containing smog the linings of their respiratory systems became damaged. People with respiratory diseases were particularly vulnerable to smog, and in the winter of 1952 5 000 people died in London. This tragedy led to the passing of laws to help reduce air pollution.

In Los Angeles, weather conditions in May to October lead to the exhaust gases from vehicles and smoke from industrial plants collecting above the city in a brown haze. Sunlight shining through this smog causes photochemical reactions to occur in it. This produces a range of chemicals including peroxyacetyl nitrate (PAN) and ozone. Both these chemicals are harmful to plants and ozone can produce asthma attacks in the people in the city.

Water pollution

Fresh water

Fresh water, such as streams and rivers, has been used from the earliest times to flush away wastes. Over the past few centuries many rivers of the world have been polluted by a wide range of industries including textile and paper making plants, tanneries and metal works. People in many countries have become aware of the dangers of pollution and laws have been passed to reduce it. Ways have been found to prevent pollution occurring and to recycle some of the materials in the wastes.

Figure 15.7 This cellulose factory is causing the water to become polluted.

7 How are the lives of people who live by polluted rivers and catch fish from them put at risk?

8 The water flowing through a village had such low levels of mercury in it that it was considered safe to drink. Many of the villagers showed signs of mercury poisoning. How could this be?

The most harmful pollutants in water are the PCBs (polychlorinated biphenyls) and heavy metals such as cadmium, chromium, nickel and lead. In large concentrations these metals damage many of the organs of the body and can cause cancers to develop. PCBs are used in making plastics and, along with mercury compounds, are taken in by living organisms at the beginning of food chains (see page 174). They are passed up the food chain as each organism is eaten by the next one along the chain. This leads to organisms at the end of the food chain having large amounts of toxic chemicals in their bodies, which can cause permanent damage or death.

The careless use of fertilisers allows them to drain from the land into the rivers and lakes and leads to the overgrowth of water plants. When these die, larger numbers of bacteria take in oxygen from water. The reduction in oxygen levels in the water kills many water animals. Phosphates in detergents also cause an overgrowth in water plants which can lead to the death of water animals in the same way.

Figure 15.8 The excessive use of fertilisers leads to algal bloom in rivers and kills fish.

Sea water

The pollutants of fresh water are washed into the sea where they may collect in the coastal marine life. The pollutants may cause damage to the plants and animals that live in the sea and make them unfit to be collected for human food.

Large amounts of oil are transported by tankers across the ocean every day. In the past the tanker crew flushed out the empty oil containers with sea water to clean them. The oil that was released from the ship formed a film on the water surface which prevented oxygen from entering the water from the air. It also reduced the amount of light that could pass through the upper waters of the sea to reach the phytoplankton and allow them to photosynthesise.

The problem of this form of oil pollution has been reduced by adopting a 'load on top' process, where the water used to clean out the containers is allowed to settle and the oil that has been collected floats to the top. This oil is kept in the tanker and is added to the next consignment of oil that is transported.

Occasionally a tanker is wrecked. When this happens large amounts of oil may spill out onto the water and be washed up onto the shore (see Figure 15.9). This causes catastropic damage to the habitat, and even with the use of detergents and the physical removal of the oil the habitat may take years to recover.

9 How does oil floating on the surface of the sea affect the organisms living under it?

Figure 15.9   Oil spills like this can have a huge effect on the sea and coastal wildlife.

Indicators of pollution

Some living things are very sensitive to pollution and therefore can be used as biological indicators of pollution.

Lichens are sensitive to air pollution. Where the air is very badly polluted no lichens grow but a bright green Protoctista called *Pleurococcus* may form a coating on trees. Crusty lichens, some species of which are yellow, can grow in air where there is some pollution. Leafy lichens grow where the air has only a little pollution. Bushy lichens can grow only in unpolluted air.

Some freshwater invertebrates can be used to estimate the amount of pollution in streams and rivers. If the water is very badly polluted there is no freshwater life, but if the water is quite badly polluted rat-tailed maggots may be present. Bloodworms can live in less badly polluted water and freshwater shrimps can live in water that has only small amounts of pollution. Stonefly nymphs can live only in unpolluted water.

Figure A Lichens.

1 How polluted is the habitat if:
   a) the trees have *Pleurococcus* and crusty yellow lichens on them?
   b) bushy, leafy and crusty lichens are found in a habitat?
   c) freshwater shrimps and bloodworms are found in a stream?
2 Four places were examined in succession along a river and the animals found there were recorded. Here are the results.
   Station A) Stonefly nymphs, mayfly nymphs, freshwater shrimp, caddis-fly larvae.
   Station B) Rat-tailed maggots, sludge worms.
   Station C) Sludge worms, bloodworms, waterlouse.
   Station D) Freshwater shrimps, waterlouse.
   What do the results show? Explain your answer.

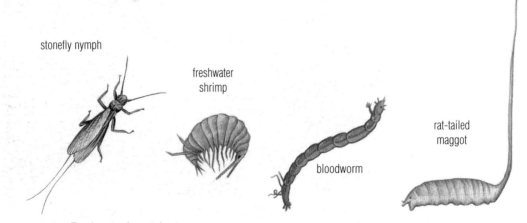

Figure B Freshwater invertebrates.

Intensive farming

As the human population has continued to grow (see page 186) ways have been found to increase food production by intensive farming. Two features of intensive farming are the use of fertilisers and pesticides.

Fertilisers

When plants are grown for food they are eventually harvested and taken out of the soil. This means that the minerals they have taken from the soil go with them to market, and there are therefore fewer minerals left in the soil for the next crop. Fertilisers are added to the soil to replace the minerals that have been taken away in the crop. They are also added in quantities that will make sure that the plants grow as healthily as possible and produce a large crop. The amount of fertiliser added to the soil has to be carefully calculated. If too little is added, the amount of food produced by the crop (called the yield) will be small. If too much is added, the plants will not use all the minerals and they may be washed into streams and rivers and cause pollution. There are two kinds of fertiliser. Inorganic fertilisers such as ammonium nitrate are manufactured chemical compounds. Organic fertilisers are made from the wastes of farm animals (manure) and humans (sewage sludge).

Figure 15.10 A helicopter spraying trees in an orchard with chemicals.

Inorganic fertilisers can give crops an almost instant supply of minerals, as the minerals dissolve in the soil water as soon as they reach it, and can be taken up by the roots straight away. The minerals in manure are released more slowly, as decomposers (see page 175) in the soil break it down.

Inorganic fertilisers are light in weight and so can be spread from aeroplanes and helicopters flying over the crops. This means that they can be applied to the crop at any time without damaging the crop. Manure is too heavy to be spread in this way and must be spread from a trailer attached to a tractor. If the manure was spread while the crop was growing the tractor and trailer would damage the crop, so the manure must instead be spread on the soil before the crop is sown. This also allows some time for the manure to release minerals into the soil.

10 What kind of fertiliser gives you the greater control over providing minerals for a crop? Explain your answer.

Fertilisers and soil structure

A good soil has particles of rock bound together with humus (decomposed plants and leaves) to form lumps called crumbs. The crumbs do not interlock but settle on each other loosely, with air spaces between them. The air provides a source of oxygen for the plant roots and for organisms living in the soil. The spaces also allow the roots to grow easily through the soil. The humus acts like a sponge and holds onto some of the water that passes through the soil. The plant roots draw on the water stored in the humus.

In time humus rots away, and in natural habitats it is replaced by the decaying bodies of other organisms. When manure is added to the soil it adds humus and this helps to bind the rock particles together and keep the soil crumbs large. If the soil receives only inorganic fertilisers the humus is gradually lost and the soil crumbs break down. The rocky fragments that remain form a dust which can be easily blown away by the wind.

11 If a farmer uses only inorganic fertilisers how may the soil organisms be affected?

Pests and pesticides

Fertilisers are used to make the crop yield as high as possible. The crop plants may however be affected by other organisms, which either compete with them for resources, or feed on them. These organisms are known as pests, and chemicals called pesticides have been developed to kill them. There are three kinds of pesticides – herbicides, fungicides and insecticides.

The problem with weeds

When a crop is sown the seeds are planted so that the plants will grow a certain distance apart from each other. This distance allows each plant to receive all the sunlight, water and minerals that it needs to grow healthily and produce a large yield.

A weed is a plant growing in the wrong place. For example, poppies may be grown in a flower bed to make a garden look attractive, but if they grow in a field of wheat they are weeds because they should not be growing there. Weeds grow in the spaces between the crop plants and compete with them for sunlight, water and minerals. This means that the crop plants may receive less sunlight because the weeds shade them, and receive less water and minerals because the weed plants take in some for their own growth. Weeds can also be infested with microbes which can cause disease in the crop plant. For example, cereals may be attacked by fungi that live on grass plants growing as weeds in the crop.

Figure 15.11 Poppies growing as weeds in a field of wheat.

12 How does the use of herbicides on a farm affect the honey production of a local bee keeper? Explain your answer.

Herbicides

Weeds are killed by herbicides. There are two kinds of herbicide – non-selective and selective. A non-selective herbicide kills any plant. It can be used to clear areas of all plant life so that crops can be grown in the soil later. It must not be used when a crop is growing as it will kill the crop plants too. A selective herbicide kills only certain plants – the weeds – and leaves the crop plants unharmed. It can be used when the crop is growing.

Herbicides may be sprayed onto crops from the air. Some of the herbicide may drift away from the field and into surrounding natural habitats. When this happens, the herbicide can kill plants there. Many wild flowers have been destroyed in this way.

Fungicides

A fungicide is a substance that kills fungi. Fungal spores may be in the soil of a crop field, floating in the air, or on the seeds before they are sown. Fungicides are coated on seeds to protect them when they germinate. They are also applied to the soil to prevent fungi attacking roots, and are sprayed on crop plants to give a protective coat against fungal spores in the air.

Insecticides

When a large number of plants of the same kind are grown together they can provide a huge feeding area for insects. Large populations of insects can build up on the plants and cause great damage. Insecticides are used to kill these insect pests. There are two kinds of insecticides – narrow spectrum and broad spectrum insecticides. Narrow spectrum insecticides are designed to kill only certain kinds of insects, and leave others unharmed. Broad spectrum insecticides in contrast kill a wide range of insects – not only those that feed on the crop, but also predatory insects which may prey on them. If insecticides drift away from the fields after spraying, they can kill other insects in their natural habitats. They can also move along the food chain.

13 You have a field of weeds and need to plant a crop in it. How could you use pesticides to prepare the ground for your crop and protect it while it is growing?

A poison in the food chain

In 1935 Paul Müller (1899–1965) set up a research programme to find a substance that would kill insects but would not harm other animals. Insects were his target because some species are plant pests and devastate farm crops, and others carry microbes that cause disease in humans. The substance also had to be cheap to make and not have an unpleasant smell. In 1939 he tried a chemical called dichlorodiphenyltrichloroethane (DDT), that was first made in 1873. DDT seemed to meet all his requirements and soon it was being used worldwide.

In time, some animals at the end of the food chains (the top carnivores) in the habitats where DDT had been sprayed to kill insects were found dead. The concentration of the DDT applied to the insects was much too weak to kill the top carnivores directly so investigations into the food chains had to be made.

In Clear Lake, California, DDT had been sprayed onto the water to kill gnat larvae. The concentration of DDT in the water was only 0.015 parts per million (ppm), but the concentration in the dead bodies of the grebes

14 Construct the food chain investigated in Clear Lake.

15 Why did the grebes die?

(fish-eating water birds) was 1600 ppm. When the planktonic organisms were examined their bodies contained 5 ppm and the small fish that fed on them contained 10 ppm.

It was discovered that DDT did not break down in the environment but was taken into living tissue and stayed there. As the plankton in the lake were eaten by the fish the DDT was taken into the fishes' bodies and built up after every meal. The small fish were eaten by larger fish in which the DDT formed higher concentrations still. The grebes ate the large fish and with every meal increased the amount of DDT in their bodies until it killed them.

In Britain, the peregrine falcon is a top carnivore in a food chain in moorland habitats, although it visits other habitats outside the breeding season. The concentration of DDT in bodies of female falcons caused them to lay eggs with weak shells. When parents incubated eggs their weight broke the shells and the embryos died.

The perfect environment for growth

When plants are grown for food, every attempt is made to ensure that the crop yield is as large as possible. Applying fertilisers helps crop growth, and the use of pesticides keeps other organisms from damaging the crop. There are however other factors that affect growth. They are the factors which affect photosynthesis – light, temperature and the amount of carbon dioxide in the air (see Chapter 11).

Figures 15.12–15.14 show how light intensity, temperature and the concentration of carbon dioxide in the air affect the rate of photosynthesis.

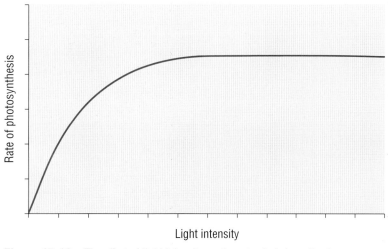

Figure 15.12   The effect of light intensity on the rate of photosynthesis.

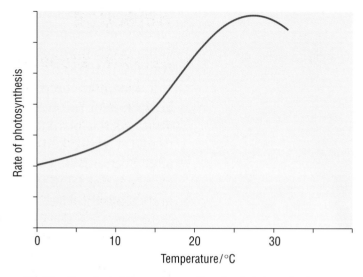

Figure 15.13   The effect of temperature on the rate of photosynthesis.

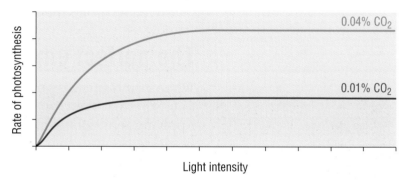

Figure 15.14   The effect of carbon dioxide concentration on the rate of photosynthesis.

Combining the three factors

The results of the experiments show that the amount of light, the temperature and the amount of carbon dioxide in the air all affect the rate of photosynthesis. This implies that the rate of photosynthesis can be increased to a maximum by carefully regulating these three factors in the environment of the plant. These factors cannot be controlled in an open field but they can be controlled by using a glasshouse.

Selection

Selective breeding

For thousands of years people have been breeding animals and plants for special purposes. Most plants were originally bred to produce more food, but later plants were also bred for decoration. Animals were originally bred for domestication, then for food production or to pull carts.

A breeding programme involves selecting organisms with the desired features and breeding them together. The variation in the offspring is examined and those with the desired feature are selected for further breeding. For example, the 'wild' form of wheat makes few grains at the top of its stalk. Individuals that produce the most grains are selected for breeding together. When their offspring are produced they are examined and the highest grain producers are selected and bred together. By following this programme wheat plants producing large numbers of grains have been developed.

Figure 15.15   'Wild' wheat (left) and modern wheat (right).

In some breeding programmes a number of features are selected and brought together. The large number of different breeds of dog have been developed in this way.

16 All the different breeds of dog have been developed from the wolf by selective breeding. What features do you think have been selected to produce a greyhound? Give a reason for each feature you mention.

Figure 15.16 A wolf and a greyhound.

Natural selection

Just as humans select individuals for further breeding, it has been found that selection in a habitat takes place naturally. Those individuals of a species which have the most suitable features to survive will continue to live and breed and pass on their features. Individuals which have features that do not equip them for survival will perish, and so do not pass on their features to future generations. This form of selection is used to explain the theory of evolution, where one species changes in time until another species is produced. The finches on the Galapagos Islands, first studied by Charles Darwin (1809–1882), are thought to have evolved by natural selection (see Figure 15.17 page 221).

For discussion

How do you think that the human species may evolve in the future?

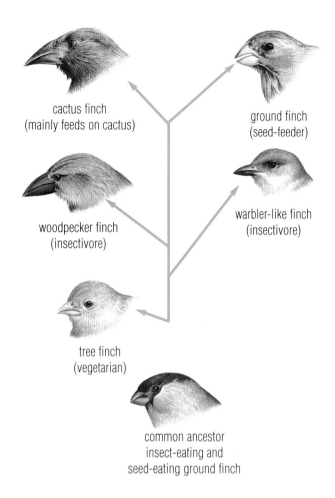

cactus finch
(mainly feeds on cactus)

ground finch
(seed-feeder)

woodpecker finch
(insectivore)

warbler-like finch
(insectivore)

tree finch
(vegetarian)

common ancestor
insect-eating and
seed-eating ground finch

Figure 15.17 Darwin's finches.

GM foods

In addition to working out the best way to grow crops, scientists also look at ways to improve the crop plants. One way to do this is by selective breeding (see page 219). A second way is by genetic modification. Food produced by plants which have been genetically modified are called GM foods. A plant is genetically modified by having genes from another organism added to it. The addition of genes may help it to grow better or help the food to be processed more cheaply. For example, some tomato plants were modified so that they produced tomatoes that made a thick tomato purée more cheaply than other kinds of tomatoes.

Genetically modified organisms are new organisms. Scientists disagree on their use because if they enter a natural habitat they may breed with organisms there to produce a more unusual organism.

1 How is genetic modification different from selective breeding?

2 Should plants such as sugar cane be genetically modified to provide fuel to replace oil? Should plants such as maize be genetically modified so they produce their own insecticides? Explain your answers.

Clones

A clone is an organism that is an exact copy of its parent. Clones can occur naturally when some organisms reproduce. *Amoeba*, a Protoctist, produces a clone by simply dividing in two.

Hydra, a small animal related to sea anemones, which lives in ponds and ditches, grows a bud which detaches itself and becomes a copy of its parent.

Some plants can also form clones. The spider plant is a familiar houseplant which grows small plants on side shoots (see page 13). The small plants can become detached and live on their own. A simple way of cloning a plant is to take a cutting from it and grow the cutting in compost to make a new plant.

For discussion

How could cloning help farming?

What disadvantages might there be to cloning farm animals?

If you were cloned today would your clone be just like you when it is your age? If not, why not?

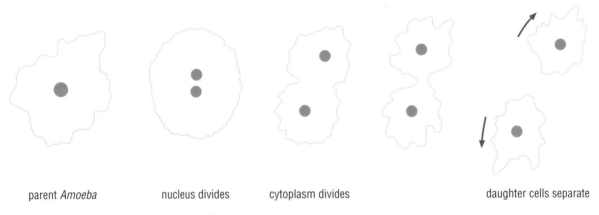

parent *Amoeba*   nucleus divides   cytoplasm divides   daughter cells separate

Figure 15.18 *Stages in the division of an* Amoeba.

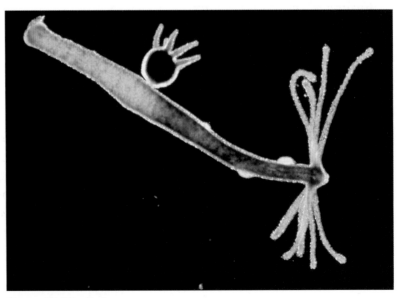

Figure 15.19 *Hydra.*

A technique for cloning animals has been developed using nuclei and cells. The nucleus is removed from an egg cell and is replaced by the nucleus of a normal body cell from the animal you wish to clone. The egg is then allowed to develop normally and an exact copy of the animal is produced. Dolly the sheep was the first successfully reared clone at the end of the 20th Century. Since then many other clones have been made.

Figure 15.20   Dolly the cloned sheep.

♦ SUMMARY ♦

- From the earliest civilisations, human activity has caused some pollution but the problem greatly increased with the Industrial Revolution (*see page 204*).
- Air is polluted by chemicals and solid particles (*see page 206*).
- Freshwater may be polluted with a range of chemicals from industry and agriculture (*see page 209*).
- Sea water may be polluted with oil (*see page 211*).
- Fertilisers provide minerals for plant growth (*see page 213*).
- Pesticides are used to kill organisms that damage crops (*see page 214*).
- Poisonous materials can be concentrated in the bodies of living things in a food chain (*see page 216*).
- Plant growth can be controlled by regulating factors such as the amount of light, heat and carbon dioxide around a plant (*see page 217*).
- New varieties of species can be produced by selective breeding (*see page 219*).
- Natural selection takes place on the organisms in a habitat. It may cause one species to change into or evolve into a new species (*see page 220*).
- A clone is an organism that is an exact copy of its parents (*see page 222*).

End of chapter question

1 Figure 15.21 shows the position of two coastal towns.

A and B are two towns that have a fishing industry. Due to over-fishing the industry has declined. There are large numbers of people now unemployed in both towns and many are thinking of moving or travelling to the cities to find work. It is proposed to build an oil refinery near one of the towns. This will bring employment for the people in the form of building and running the refinery, and in the factories that may be set up to use its products. Land will be needed for the refinery

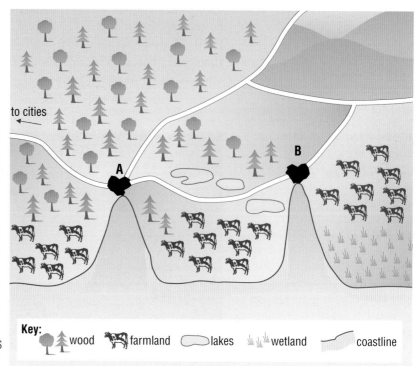

Figure 15.21   Map showing positions of towns A and B.

and for the port where the oil tankers will dock. Land will also be needed for factories and perhaps housing estates if more people come to live in the town.

a) What else may land be needed for if more people come to the town?

b) What habitats may be affected by the building of the oil refinery? Explain your answers.

For discussion

What are the advantages and disadvantages of choosing to build the refinery near town A or B?

What are the major issues involved in deciding where the refinery is to be built?

How would you balance these issues to decide which town is best suited for the refinery and the port?

For discussion

Imagine that you are going to live on an island with about two dozen other people. The island has four seasons, with a warm summer and a cool winter. It has a hill near its centre which provides some shelter from the cold prevailing wind. Much of the low land on the sheltered side of the hill is woodland. There is a small population of fish in the sea around the island which can provide a little food. Work out a plan for providing food for yourself and the rest of the group for a stay of 2 years on the island. You may take any plants, animals, pesticides, fertilisers and building materials that you wish, and you may begin your stay on the island in any season.

Glossary

Some of the words in this glossary are green. These are words which feature in the wordlists of the Cambridge Checkpoint Science (Biology) Scheme of Work.

A

acid rain   Rain that has been acidified by reacting with certain chemicals in the air produced by power stations and car exhausts.

adaptation   The way a living thing is suited to its habitat so that it can survive there. Adaptation can also mean the process by which living things become more suited to their habitat.

alimentary canal   The digestive tube that begins with the mouth and ends with the anus. It is also sometimes called the gut.

amino acid   A molecule containing carbon, hydrogen, oxygen and nitrogen. It links up with other amino acids to form long-chain molecules called proteins.

anaemia   An unhealthy condition that may be due to the lack of iron in the diet. One of the symptoms is tiredness.

antagonistic muscles   A pair of muscles in which each of the contracting muscles brings about a movement that is opposite in direction to the other.

anther   The organ in a flower that produces pollen grains.

artery   A blood vessel with elastic walls that carries blood away from the heart.

arthropods   Animals with a jointed skeleton on the outside of the bodies which allows them to move their limbs.

B

bacteria   Organisms with the body of only one cell. Some feed on wastes in soil while a few feed and breed inside the human body, and cause disease.

bile   A substance made by the liver and stored in the gall bladder. It is released onto food in the duodenum to aid the digestion of fats.

biomass   The mass of an organism or group of organisms after their bodies have been dried out.

breathing   The movement of air in and out of the lungs. In fish, breathing means the movement of water in and out of the cavity which contains the lungs.

C

calyx   The ring of sepals in a flower.

capillary   A blood vessel with one-cell-thick walls through which substances pass between the blood and the surrounding cells.

carbohydrate   A nutrient made from carbon, hydrogen and oxygen. Most are made by plants.

carnivore   An animal that eats only other animals for food.

carpel   The female organ of a flower that produces the fruit and the seed.

cell (in biology)   The basic unit of life. The cell contains a nucleus, cytoplasm and membrane around the outside. The bodies of most living things are made from large numbers of cells.

cell membrane   A very thin sheet of material which surrounds the cytoplasm in a cell.

cell wall   A layer made from cellulose which encloses the cell membrane in plant cells.

chlorophyll   A green pigment found mainly in plant cells that traps energy from sunlight and makes it available for the process of photosynthesis.

chloroplast   A component of a cell. It is green and absorbs some of the energy of sunlight for use in photosynthesis.

chromosome   A thread-like structure that appears when the cell nucleus divides. It contains DNA.

cilia   Short hair-like projections that may form on the surface of a cell. They can beat to and fro to move the bodies of Protoctista or to help with the movement of fluids in animal systems.

circulation   The regular movement of a fluid around a particular area such as blood flowing around the body.

clone   One of a number of identical individuals produced by asexual reproduction.

combustion   A chemical reaction in which a substance reacts quickly with oxygen and heat is given out in the process. If a flame is produced, burning is said to take place.

consumer   An animal that eats either plants or other animals.

corolla   The ring of petals in a flower.

cotyledon   A leaf on the tiny plant inside a seed.

cross-pollination   The transfer of pollen from the anthers of a flower on one plant to the stigma of a flower on another plant of the same species.

cytoplasm   A fluid-like substance in the cell in which processes take place to keep the cell alive.

D

deciduous   A feature of plants which shed their leaves at the end of each growing season.

deficiency   Having an insufficient amount of something.

diet   The food that a human or animal normally eats. In the case of humans, this may be a healthy or unhealthy diet.

GLOSSARY

digestion   The process of breaking down large food particles into small ones so that they can be absorbed by the body.

dispersal   The spreading out of living things, especially seeds, so that they do not compete with each other for resources such as light and food.

DNA (deoxyribonucleic acid)   A substance in the nuclei of cells that contains information, in the form of a code, about how an organism should develop and function.

E

ecology   The study of living things in their natural surroundings or habitat.

ecosystem   An ecological system in which the different species in a community react with each other and with the non-living environment. Ecosystems are found in all habitats such as lakes and woods.

egestion (*see also* excretion)   The release of undigested food and other contents of the alimentary canal from the anus.

enzyme   A chemical made by a cell that is used to speed up chemical reactions in life processes such as digestion and respiration.

excrete   The action taken by an organism to release waste products made by chemical reactions inside the body.

excretion (*see also* egestion)   The release of waste products made by chemical reactions inside the body.

F

fats   Food substances that provide energy. They belong to a group of substances called lipids, which include oils and waxes.

feed   To take food into the body.

fertilisation   The fusion of the nuclei from the male and female gametes that results in the formation of a zygote.

fertiliser   Manufactured substances which are given to plants to maximise their growth.

food chain   A number of organisms arranged in a series. Each one is the series is eaten by the next one in the series.

food web   The way a number of food chains in a habitat link together to show how food and energy pass through the habitat.

fruit   A structure that forms from the ovary of a flowering plant after fertilisation has taken place.

function   The way something works to fulfil a purpose. For example, the function of the circulatory system is to move blood around the body.

fungi   Organisms which possess a material called chitin and reproduce by making spores and feed by releasing a digestive juice onto the food around them. Mushrooms and yeast are fungi.

G

gene   A section of DNA that contains the information about how a particular characteristic, such as hair colour or eye colour, can develop in the organism.

genetic engineering   The process of moving genes between different types of organisms to produce new organisms with particularly useful properties.

genetic material   Material in the nucleus of a cell which is made of genes.

germination   The process in which the plant inside a seed begins to grow and bursts out of the seed coat.

greenhouse effect   The way gases in the atmosphere such as carbon dioxide trap heat radiating from the Earth, like the way that glass traps heat radiating from the inside of a greenhouse.

greenhouse gas   A gas in the atmosphere which prevents heat radiating from the Earth from passing into space.

growth   Increase in size and complexity.

H

habitat   The place where a particular living thing survives.

haemoglobin   The pigment in red blood cells that contains iron and transports oxygen around the body.

herbivore   An animal that eats only plants for food.

I

invertebrates   Animals without a spine or backbone.

K

key   A series of statements which can be used with observations on an organism to identify it.

keystone species   A species on which many other species in a habitat depend for their survival.

L

life cycle   A description of the changes which take place in an organism during its life.

M

magnification   The power of a microscope to provide an enlarged or magnified view of a specimen.

microbes   Living things which are too small to be seen without the aid of a microscope.

microscope   A scientific instrument which gives an enlarged or magnified view of a specimen such as a group of cells.

mineral (in biology)   A substance taken up from the soil water by the plant roots and used for growth and development of the plant. It is also an essential nutrient in the diet of animals.

movement   Change of position.

N

natural selection   The process by which evolution is thought to take place. Individuals in a species best suited to an environment will thrive there and produce more offspring, while less well suited individuals will produce fewer offspring. In time the less well suited will die out leaving the best suited individuals to form a new species.

nerve   A cord-like structure which is composed of groups of nerve cell fibres.

nucleus (in biology)   The part of the cell that contains the DNA and controls the activities and development of the cell.

nutrient   A substance in a food that provides a living thing with material for growth, development and good health.

nutrition   The process in which nutrients are provided for the body. For example, good nutrition makes a healthy diet.

O

omnivore   An animal that eats both plants and animals for food.

organ   A part of the body, made from a group of cell tissues, that performs an important function in the life of the organism.

organ system   A group of organs that work together to perform a major task in keeping the body alive. For example, the stomach, liver, pancreas and intestines are organs that form the digestive system.

organism   A living thing made from just one cell or from many cells.

ovary   The organ where the female gametes are made in plants and animals.

P

peristalsis   The wave of muscular contraction that moves food along the alimentary canal.

pest   An organism which when present in large numbers destroys a crop or greatly reduces the production of food.

phloem   A living tissue in a plant through which food made in the leaves passes to all parts of the plant.

photosynthesis   The process by which plants make carbohydrates and oxygen from water and carbon dioxide, using the energy from light that has been trapped in chlorophyll.

pistil   A structure made from a group of carpels.

pollen   Microscopic grains produced by the anther, which contain the male gamete for sexual reproduction in flowering plants.

pollination   The transfer of pollen from an anther to a stigma.

pollution   Large amounts of waste substances that contaminate the air, water and land.

predator   An animal which feeds or preys on another animal.

prey   An animal which is eaten by or falls prey to a predator.

producer   An organism that produces food at the start of a food chain.

protein   A substance made from amino acids. Proteins are used to build many structures in the bodies of living things.

R

reproduction   Production of new members of a species.

respiration   The process in which energy is released from food.

S

saliva   A watery substance produced by glands in the mouth that makes food easier to swallow and begins the digestion of carbohydrates.

scientific method   A series of processes used by scientists to perform investigations and make discoveries.

season   A time of year when certain environmental conditions occur, for example, the dry season.

seed   A structure that forms from the ovule after fertilisation. It contains the embryo plant and a food store.

selection   A process which acts on living things through the genes and conditions in the environment to produce organisms which are best suited to survive in their surroundings.

selective breeding   Selecting organisms with desired features and breeding them together to produce offspring with even stronger desired features. For example, wheat with very large grains has been developed from wheat with large grains by selective breeding.

self-pollination   The transfer of pollen from the anthers to the stigma of the same flower.

sensitive   Able to detect changes in the environment.

sepal   A leaf-like structure that protects a flower when it is in bud.

species   A group of living things which have very similar features and can breed together to produce offspring also capable of breeding.

stamen   A structure in a flower composed of the anther and the filament.

stigma   The region on a carpel on which pollen grains are trapped.

T

tissue   A structure made from large numbers of one type of cell.

GLOSSARY

U

urea A chemical made when amino acids are broken down in the body to make a carbohydrate called glycogen. It is excreted by the kidneys.

urine A watery solution that contains urea.

V

vacuole A large cavity in a plant cell that is filled with a watery solution called cell sap. May also occur as small, fluid-filled cavities in some animal cells and some Protoctista.

variation A feature that varies among individuals of the same species, such as height or hair colour.

vein A thin-walled blood vessel that transports blood towards the heart.

vertebrates Animals with a spine or backbone.

vitamin A substance made by plants and animals that is an essential component of the diet to keep the body in good health.

X

xylem The non-living tissue in a plant through which the water and minerals pass from the root through to the shoot.

Index

Note: page numbers in *italics* refer to entries in the Glossary.